Echoes of Tomorrow

AI and the Future of Society

Copyright © 2024 by RK Books

All rights reserved.

No part of this publication may be reproduced, distributed, or transmitted in any form or by any means, including photocopying, recording, or other electronic or mechanical methods, without the prior written permission of the publisher, except in the case of brief quotations embodied in critical reviews and certain other noncommercial uses permitted by copyright law.

This book is a work of fiction. Names, characters, places, and incidents are products of the author's imagination or are used fictitiously. Any resemblance to actual events, locales, or persons, living or dead, is entirely coincidental.

Published by |

Table of Cotents

Chapter 1 The Foundations of Artificial Intelligence 1

    The Evolution of AI: From Theory to Reality 2

    Key Technologies Driving AI 4

Chapter 2 AI in Everyday Life 8

    Smart Homes and Personal Assistants 9

    AI in Healthcare: Diagnosis and Treatment 11

    The Impact of AI on Education 14

Chapter 3 AI in the Business World 18

    Revolutionizing Industries with AI 18

    AI in Marketing and Customer Experience 21

    The Future of Work: AI and Automation 25

Chapter 4 Ethical Considerations and AI 26

    The Ethics of AI: Privacy, Bias, and Control 27

    AI Governance and Policy Making 29

Chapter 5 AI and the Global Society 34

    AI in Developing Countries 34

    The Role of AI in Environmental Sustainability 38

Chapter 6 The Future of AI Technology 42

    Emerging Trends in AI Research 42

    Potential Breakthroughs and Their Implications 46

Chapter 7 Preparing for an AI Future 50

    Education and Skill Development for an AI Era 51

    Shaping Policies for an AI-Driven World 54

Chapter 8 Dystopia or Utopia? Contrasting Visions of AI's Impact 58

Optimistic Views on AI and Society 59

Pessimistic Scenarios and Concerns 62

Chapter 9 AI in Art and Creativity 66

AI's Role in Music, Visual Arts, and Literature 66

The Future of Creative Work in an AI World 69

AI as a Collaborative Partner in Creative Processes 72

The Ethics and Aesthetics of AI-Generated Art 76

Chapter 10 AI and Space Exploration 80

AI in Navigating the Cosmos 81

The Role of AI in Future Space Missions 84

AI in Astrobiology and Extraterrestrial Research 87

AI-Powered Robotics in Space Exploration 90

Chapter 11 AI and the Future of Governance 95

AI in Public Administration and Services 95

The Impact of AI on Global Politics and Diplomacy 98

AI in Law Enforcement and Judicial Systems 101

AI and the Future of Democratic Processes 104

Chapter 12 AI in Personal Development and Self-Improvement 108

AI as a Tool for Personal Growth 109

The Future of Personalized Learning and Self-Optimization 112

AI in Fitness and Wellness: Enhancing Health and Well-being 118

AI and the Quest for Life Balance: Leveraging Technology for Well-being
.... 120

Chapter 1
The Foundations of Artificial Intelligence

In this inaugural chapter, we embark on a journey to understand the bedrock of Artificial Intelligence (AI) a technology that stands at the cusp of reshaping our world. From its conceptual beginnings in the mid-20th century, AI has evolved from mere science fiction into a tangible force driving modern innovation. This evolution has been fueled by leaps in computational power, breakthroughs in algorithms, and an ever-expanding digital universe.

We delve into the historical timeline of AI, tracing its roots from the early dreams of automatons and logical machines, through the winter periods of skepticism and underfunding, to the current renaissance marked by machine learning and deep learning breakthroughs. This exploration is not just a chronicle of technological advancements but also a narrative of the human intellect and ambition that propels this field forward.

Understanding AI's foundations requires a look at key technologies such as neural networks, natural language processing, and robotics, each a cog in the larger AI machinery. As we unfold the layers of AI's development, we'll see how it has become intertwined with our daily lives, transforming industries and sparking ethical debates. This chapter sets the stage for an in-depth discussion on how AI is not only a technological marvel but a mirror reflecting our societal values and future aspirations.

The Evolution of AI: From Theory to Reality

The story of Artificial Intelligence (AI) is a fascinating saga of human ingenuity and relentless pursuit of understanding intelligence. This narrative takes us from the theoretical constructs of early philosophers and mathematicians to today's sophisticated AI systems, impacting almost every aspect of our lives.

Theoretical Beginnings and Early Concepts (1950s 1970s)

AI's journey began in the realm of philosophy and mathematics. Ancient philosophers like Aristotle and Plato pondered the nature of intelligence and reasoning, setting the stage for future explorations. However, it wasn't until the mid-20th century that AI emerged as a distinct field. The 1956 Dartmouth Conference, often cited as AI's birthplace, saw luminaries like John McCarthy and Marvin Minsky gather to discuss the possibility of creating machines that could simulate human intelligence.

In these early years, AI research focused on developing basic algorithms and problem-solving techniques. One of the earliest successes was the creation of rule-based systems, exemplified by programs like the Logic Theorist and ELIZA. These systems, albeit primitive, demonstrated that machines could execute tasks that, if performed by humans, would require intelligence.

The First AI Winter (1970s mid-1980s)

Despite initial excitement, the field encountered its first major setback, now known as the 'AI Winter.' During this period, the limitations of early AI became apparent. The computational power needed to process complex algorithms was lacking, and funding for AI research dwindled. This period was marked by skepticism and a reassessment of the overly optimistic expectations that had been set for AI.

The Rise of Machine Learning (mid-1980s 2000s)

The revival of AI came with the advent of machine learning, a paradigm shift from hard-coded programming to systems that could learn from data. The development of algorithms like backpropagation for neural networks in the 1980s played a pivotal role in this resurgence. These methods enabled computers to adjust their operations based on the data they processed, mimicking the learning process of the human brain to some extent.

During this era, AI began to demonstrate its practical value. One of the notable achievements was IBM's Deep Blue, a chess-playing computer that defeated world champion Garry Kasparov in 1997, showcasing the potential of AI in solving complex problems.

The Boom of Deep Learning and Big Data (2000s Present)

The explosion of digital data in the 21st century, combined with significant advances in computational power and storage, paved the way for the current era of AI. Deep learning, a subset of machine learning involving neural networks with many layers, became the driving force behind AI's recent successes. This era has seen AI breakthroughs in image and speech recognition, natural language processing, and autonomous systems.

Notable developments include Google's AlphaGo, which defeated the world Go champion in 2016, and the widespread use of AI in personal assistants like Amazon's Alexa and Apple's Siri. AI's capabilities have expanded into sectors such as healthcare for disease diagnosis, finance for algorithmic trading, and autonomous vehicles.

Ethical Considerations and Future Directions

As AI becomes more ingrained in our lives, it raises important ethical and societal questions. Issues like data privacy, algorithmic bias, and the future of employment in an automated world are hot topics of debate. The challenge lies in harnessing AI's potential while ensuring it's developed and used responsibly.

Looking ahead, AI is poised to become even more integrated into our daily lives. Future advancements may lead to AI systems with better understanding and interaction capabilities, further blurring the lines between human and machine intelligence. There's also growing interest in achieving Artificial General Intelligence (AGI), where AI would possess the ability to understand, learn, and apply its intelligence broadly, akin to human cognitive abilities.

The evolution of AI from theory to reality is a testament to human curiosity and technological advancement. From its humble beginnings to its current state, AI has not only transformed the technological landscape but also revolutionized how we perceive intelligence and the potential of machines. As we stand on the brink of further groundbreaking developments, it is imperative to consider the ethical implications and strive for a future where AI benefits all of humanity.

Key Technologies Driving AI

Artificial Intelligence (AI) has seen unprecedented growth and evolution, primarily driven by key technologies that have acted as catalysts in its advancement. These technologies not only form the backbone of current AI systems but also shape the future trajectory of this dynamic field.

Machine Learning: The Heart of AI

Central to AI's progress is Machine Learning (ML), a technique enabling computers to learn from and make predictions or decisions based on data. Unlike traditional programming, where tasks are explicitly programmed, ML algorithms allow systems to learn and improve from experience automatically. This shift is fundamental to

AI's ability to handle complex, variable tasks such as image recognition, language processing, and predictive analytics.

Deep Learning: Mimicking the Human Brain

A subset of ML, Deep Learning (DL), has been pivotal in recent AI breakthroughs. It involves neural networks with multiple layers (hence "deep") that can learn and make intelligent decisions. Inspired by the structure and function of the human brain, these deep neural networks can analyze vast amounts of data with a level of complexity and subtlety not achievable by simpler ML models. This technology is the driving force behind voice-controlled assistants, sophisticated image recognition systems, and autonomous vehicles.

Natural Language Processing: Bridging AI and Human Language

Natural Language Processing (NLP) allows AI systems to understand, interpret, and respond to human language in a meaningful way. It encompasses everything from speech recognition to sentiment analysis. Advancements in NLP have been crucial in the development of chatbots, translation services, and personal assistants. The ability to process and analyze large volumes of text data has also opened up applications in areas like market analysis and healthcare.

Reinforcement Learning: Learning through Interaction

Another vital technology in AI is Reinforcement Learning (RL), where an AI system learns to make decisions by performing actions and observing the results. This trial-and-error approach, guided by rewards or penalties, is instrumental in areas where explicit programming is not feasible, such as in complex games (like Go or Chess) or in developing efficient strategies for resource management.

Computer Vision: Enabling Machines to See

Computer Vision enables machines to interpret and make decisions based on visual data from the world. By processing images or videos, AI systems can identify and classify objects, detect and interpret human behavior, and even generate visual content. This technology is fundamental in applications ranging from facial recognition systems and medical image analysis to real-time video surveillance.

Robotics: AI in Physical Form

Robotics, when integrated with AI, extends intelligence into the physical world. AI-driven robots can perform complex tasks, adapt to their environments, and learn from their experiences. This convergence has significant implications in manufacturing, logistics, healthcare (surgical robots, for example), and even in personal robots.

Edge AI: Processing at the Source

Edge AI refers to AI algorithms that are processed locally on a hardware device. It enables real-time data processing without needing constant connectivity to a centralized server. This technology is critical in applications where speed and privacy are paramount, such as in autonomous vehicles or in IoT (Internet of Things) devices.

Quantum Computing: The Future Frontier

Though still in its nascent stages, Quantum Computing holds immense potential for AI. Quantum computers, with their ability to handle vast amounts of data and run complex models much faster than classical computers, could revolutionize AI algorithms' efficiency and capabilities.

These key technologies underpinning AI are not just standalone developments; they often intersect and amplify each other's capabilities. For instance, deep learning improves NLP, and robotics becomes more adaptable with ML. As these technologies continue to advance, they will unlock new AI capabilities, paving the way for more innovative applications and fundamentally changing how we interact with technology. The future of AI, driven by these technologies, promises to be as exciting as it is transformative, holding the potential to redefine the limits of what machines can achieve.

Chapter 2

AI in Everyday Life

In Chapter 2, we turn our focus to the realms where Artificial Intelligence has seamlessly woven itself into the fabric of everyday life. This integration is so subtle and pervasive that often, we interact with AI without even realizing it. From the moment we wake up to the time we retire for the night, AI is there, enhancing, simplifying, and sometimes complicating our daily routines.

AI's presence is felt in our homes, where smart devices anticipate our needs and preferences, adjusting lighting, temperature, and even suggesting recipes based on our health goals. Our virtual assistants, powered by sophisticated AI algorithms, respond to our commands, help manage our schedules, and keep us connected to the world. In healthcare, AI assists in early diagnosis and personalized treatment plans, demonstrating its life-saving potential.

As we navigate through our day, AI continues to influence our experiences from the curated content we consume on social media to the recommendations on e-commerce platforms, and the route navigation in our cars. This chapter explores the omnipresence of AI in our daily activities, shedding light on how it has revolutionized communication, entertainment, shopping, and more. The silent yet impactful role of AI in everyday life reflects a profound shift in our interaction with technology, marking a new era in the human-digital coexistence.

Smart Homes and Personal Assistants

In the realm of Artificial Intelligence, smart homes and personal assistants represent a significant leap forward in how we interact with technology in our daily lives. These advancements aren't just about convenience; they're about creating a more intuitive, responsive, and personalized living experience.

The Rise of Smart Homes

The concept of a 'smart home' is centered around automation, efficiency, and personalization, all powered by AI. The integration of AI in home technology has led to an ecosystem of interconnected devices that communicate with each other and adapt to the homeowner's lifestyle.

Intelligent Climate Control: AI-driven thermostats like Nest learn from your habits and preferences. They adjust your home's temperature based on your schedule, the weather, and even your past preferences, optimizing comfort and energy efficiency.

Advanced Security Systems: AI has revolutionized home security. Systems now feature facial recognition, unusual activity detection, and real-time alerts to homeowners. AI algorithms can differentiate between residents, visitors, pets, and potential intruders, providing a nuanced approach to home security.

AI in Kitchen Appliances: From refrigerators that track food expiry dates and suggest recipes based on ingredients, to ovens that automatically adjust cooking times and temperatures, AI in kitchen appliances is about convenience and efficiency.

Smart Lighting and Energy Management: AI-enabled lighting systems adjust the brightness and color temperature based on the time of day, occupancy, or even the mood of the occupants. Similarly, AI in energy management ensures that electricity usage is optimized, reducing wastage and costs.

Automated Cleaning Devices: Robotic vacuum cleaners and mops are now commonplace. These devices map your home and clean efficiently, learning over time to optimize their cleaning patterns.

The Evolution of Personal Assistants

The transformation from simple voice-recognition software to AI-powered personal assistants marks a significant evolution in user interaction with technology. Personal assistants like Amazon's Alexa, Apple's Siri, and Google Assistant are becoming more than just tools; they are evolving into AI companions integrated into our daily lives.

Voice and Language Recognition: At their core, these assistants use Natural Language Processing (NLP) to understand and respond to voice commands. This technology has advanced to the point where these assistants can recognize different voices, understand context, and even detect emotions to some extent.

Daily Scheduling and Reminders: Personal assistants can manage calendars, set reminders, and even suggest the best times for meetings based on your schedule. They can provide traffic updates, suggest departure times, and integrate with other smart devices to streamline your daily routine.

Information and Entertainment Hub: These assistants provide news updates, play music, and control streaming services. They can read audiobooks, answer queries, and even engage in casual conversation, becoming a central hub for both information and entertainment.

Home Automation Control: Personal assistants are increasingly becoming the central control points for other smart home devices. They can control lighting, adjust thermostats, manage security systems, and interact with a wide range of IoT devices.

Health and Wellness Monitoring: Some personal assistants are now capable of providing health and wellness monitoring, offering reminders to take medication, suggesting workout routines, and even tracking sleep patterns.

Challenges and Ethical Considerations

As we embrace the conveniences offered by smart homes and personal assistants, it's crucial to consider the challenges and ethical implications. Privacy concerns are paramount, as these devices collect vast amounts of personal data. Ensuring the security of this data against breaches is a significant challenge. Additionally, there's the issue of digital divide; as these technologies become more integrated into daily life, there's a risk of widening the gap between those who have access to them and those who don't.

The infiltration of AI into our homes and daily routines through smart home technology and personal assistants represents a profound shift in our interaction with our living spaces and technology. These AI-driven systems not only offer unprecedented convenience and efficiency but also raise important questions about privacy, security, and equity. As we continue to advance technologically, it's vital to balance these benefits with responsible usage and ethical considerations.

AI in Healthcare: Diagnosis and Treatment

Artificial Intelligence (AI) in healthcare represents one of the most significant technological advancements in recent times. Its impact on diagnosis and treatment is reshaping the medical landscape, offering groundbreaking solutions and improving patient care. This detailed exploration delves into how AI is revolutionizing these critical areas of healthcare.

Revolutionizing Diagnosis with AI

AI's role in diagnosis is characterized by increased accuracy, speed, and efficiency.

Medical Imaging and Radiology: AI algorithms excel at analyzing complex imaging data. They can detect anomalies in X-rays, MRIs, and CT scans more quickly and accurately than human eyes. For instance, AI systems can identify early signs of diseases such as cancer, osteoporosis, or neurological disorders, often before they become apparent to clinicians.

Pathology: In pathology, AI helps in analyzing tissue samples, detecting abnormalities that indicate diseases like cancer. By rapidly processing and interpreting vast amounts of data, AI reduces the time taken for diagnosis, allowing for quicker treatment initiation.

Predictive Analytics: AI-driven predictive analytics use patient data to foresee potential health issues before they manifest. By analyzing patterns in historical and real-time data, these systems can predict risks for conditions like heart disease, diabetes, or chronic kidney disease, enabling preventive measures.

Genomics and Personalized Medicine: AI's ability to process vast genomic data sets is paving the way for personalized medicine. By understanding a patient's genetic makeup, AI can predict the risk of genetic disorders and recommend personalized treatment plans.

Enhancing Treatment with AI

AI not only assists in diagnosis but also plays a crucial role in treatment, offering more personalized and effective care.

Treatment Planning: AI algorithms analyze medical records, research data, and treatment outcomes to suggest the most effective treatment plans. For complex conditions like cancer, AI can recommend a combination of treatments (like surgery, chemotherapy, and radiation) tailored to the patient's unique profile.

Drug Development and Precision Medicine: AI accelerates the drug development process by predicting how different drugs will interact with diseases at a molecular level. This approach is fundamental in developing precision medicine, where treatments are tailored to individual genetic profiles, lifestyles, and environments.

Robotic Surgery: In the operating room, AI-driven robotic systems assist surgeons in performing complex procedures with high precision and control. These systems enhance a surgeon's capabilities, allowing for minimally invasive procedures, reduced recovery times, and improved patient outcomes.

Virtual Health Assistants and Telemedicine: AI-powered virtual health assistants provide continuous support and monitoring for patients, especially those with chronic conditions. They remind patients to take medication, track health metrics, and provide health information. Telemedicine platforms, enhanced with AI, offer remote diagnostics and consultations, crucial in areas with limited access to healthcare facilities.

AI in Mental Health

AI also extends its capabilities to mental health care. It provides tools for early detection of mental health issues by analyzing speech patterns, facial expressions, and writing styles. AI-driven chatbots and therapy apps offer cognitive behavioral therapy and emotional support, making mental health care more accessible.

Challenges and Ethical Considerations

Despite the potential, integrating AI into healthcare faces challenges. Ensuring data privacy and security is paramount, as healthcare data is highly sensitive. Addressing algorithmic biases that may arise from training AI on limited or skewed datasets is crucial to avoid discriminatory practices in healthcare.

Moreover, the deployment of AI in healthcare raises ethical questions around patient consent, transparency of AI-driven decisions, and the potential replacement of human judgment in critical healthcare decisions.

AI's integration into healthcare diagnosis and treatment marks a new era in medicine. It brings enhanced accuracy, efficiency, and personalized care, potentially transforming patient outcomes. However, its successful implementation hinges on addressing technological, ethical, and regulatory challenges. As AI continues to evolve, its symbiotic relationship with healthcare professionals will likely become more robust, leading to an era where AI and human expertise work hand in hand for the betterment of patient care and overall health outcomes.

The Impact of AI on Education

The integration of Artificial Intelligence (AI) in education is transforming the landscape of learning and teaching. Its impact is multifaceted, bringing innovations that personalize learning experiences, enhance teaching methods, and streamline administrative processes. In this detailed examination, we explore how AI is reshaping education.

Personalized Learning Experiences

Adaptive Learning Systems: AI-powered adaptive learning technologies offer a personalized educational journey for each student. These systems analyze students' learning styles, strengths, and weaknesses, adapting in real-time to provide customized resources and activities. This approach ensures that students receive support tailored to their individual needs, enhancing their learning outcomes.

Tutoring Systems: AI-driven tutoring systems can simulate one-on-one interaction between students and a tutor. They provide immediate feedback, clarify doubts, and guide students through complex concepts at their own pace, filling gaps in understanding that might occur in a traditional classroom setting.

Enhancing Teaching Methods

Data-Driven Insights for Teachers: AI tools analyze classroom data to offer insights to teachers about students' learning progress and engagement levels. This information helps educators tailor their teaching strategies to better address the needs of their students.

Augmented and Virtual Reality (AR/VR): AI-enhanced AR and VR technologies create immersive learning experiences, making abstract concepts tangible. For example, students can virtually travel through the human circulatory system or explore historical sites, enhancing their understanding and retention of complex subjects.

Streamlining Administrative Tasks

Automated Grading and Assessment: AI can automate the grading of assignments and assessments, particularly for objective type questions. This not only saves time for educators but also allows for timely feedback to students, a crucial aspect of the learning process.

Efficient School Management: AI systems streamline various administrative tasks such as scheduling, student enrollment, and record-keeping. By automating these processes, educational institutions can operate more efficiently and allocate more resources to teaching and learning.

AI in Curriculum Development and Content Delivery

Dynamic Curriculum Design: AI algorithms can assist in designing dynamic curricula that evolve based on emerging trends, student performance data, and feedback. This approach ensures that educational content remains relevant and effective.

Interactive and Engaging Content: AI-driven platforms offer interactive and multimedia-rich educational content, making learning more engaging and accessible. These platforms often include games, simulations, and interactive quizzes, catering to diverse learning preferences.

Overcoming Educational Barriers

Language Translation and Accessibility: AI-powered translation tools break down language barriers, providing access to educational materials in multiple languages. This feature is particularly beneficial for non-native speakers and contributes to educational equity.

Support for Special Needs: AI technologies offer customized learning solutions for students with special needs. For example, speech-to-text and text-to-speech functionalities aid students with hearing or visual impairments, while AI-driven programs can help those with learning disabilities by adapting content to their learning pace and style.

The Future of AI in Education: Opportunities and Challenges

AI's potential in education is vast, yet its implementation is not without challenges. One major concern is the digital divide; disparities in access to technology can widen educational inequalities. Additionally, the reliance on AI in education raises questions about data privacy and the need for safeguards to protect sensitive student information.

Moreover, the role of teachers in an AI-driven education system needs careful consideration. While AI can augment the teaching process, it cannot replace the human element crucial for students' emotional and social development. Educators must be equipped with the necessary skills to integrate AI tools into their teaching practices effectively.

AI's impact on education is profound and far-reaching. It promises to revolutionize how we learn, teach, and manage educational systems. By personalizing learning experiences, enhancing teaching methods, and streamlining administrative tasks, AI is not just changing the face of education; it is making it more accessible, efficient, and inclusive. As we embrace these technological advancements, it is imperative to address the accompanying challenges and ensure that AI in education serves as a tool for empowerment and equitable access to quality education for all.

Chapter 3
AI in the Business World

In Chapter 3, we delve into the transformative role of Artificial Intelligence in the business world. AI's impact on businesses is profound and far-reaching, heralding a new era of innovation, efficiency, and competitiveness. Across industries, from small startups to multinational corporations, AI is not just a luxury but a crucial driver of growth and sustainability.

This influence of AI in business is multifaceted. It enhances customer experiences, optimizes operations, and offers unprecedented insights into market trends and consumer behavior. In retail, AI personalizes shopping experiences and streamlines supply chains. In finance, it powers algorithmic trading and risk management. Manufacturing sees AI optimizing production lines and predictive maintenance, while in marketing, AI's ability to analyze vast datasets transforms how companies understand and engage with their customers.

However, the integration of AI in business is not without its challenges. It raises questions about job displacement, ethical use of consumer data, and the need for new skill sets in the workforce. This chapter aims to explore these diverse aspects, illustrating how AI is reshaping the business landscape, its potential benefits, and the challenges that need addressing to harness its full potential.

Revolutionizing Industries with AI

Artificial Intelligence (AI) is not just an emerging technological trend; it is a powerful force revolutionizing industries across the globe. Its capacity to learn, adapt, and optimize has led to transformative changes in how industries operate, compete, and innovate. This detailed examination delves into how AI is reshaping various sectors.

Manufacturing: Efficiency and Precision

In manufacturing, AI brings unprecedented efficiency and precision. Smart factories, equipped with AI-driven robotics, are revolutionizing production lines. These robots perform tasks with high precision and speed, reducing errors and increasing output. AI also plays a crucial role in predictive maintenance, analyzing data from machinery to predict and prevent breakdowns, thereby reducing downtime and maintenance costs.

Additionally, AI-driven supply chain management optimizes inventory, forecasts demand, and identifies the most efficient logistics routes. This intelligent supply chain management not only cuts costs but also improves customer satisfaction through timely deliveries.

Healthcare: Improved Diagnosis and Personalized Treatment

AI's impact in healthcare is transformative, particularly in diagnosis and personalized treatment. Machine learning algorithms analyse medical images with greater accuracy and speed than human radiologists, leading to earlier and more accurate diagnoses. In drug discovery, AI accelerates the process of identifying potential drugs and predicting their effectiveness, significantly reducing the time and cost of bringing new drugs to market.

AI also enables personalized medicine, tailoring treatments to individual patients based on their genetic makeup, lifestyle, and other factors. This approach promises more effective treatment with fewer side effects.

Finance: Smarter Decision-Making and Fraud Prevention

In finance, AI is reshaping how businesses and consumers manage money. AI-driven algorithmic trading analyzes vast amounts of financial data to make trading decisions at speeds and volumes impossible for humans. This technology enables more efficient markets and potentially higher returns.

AI also plays a crucial role in fraud detection. By learning to spot patterns in transactions that may indicate fraudulent activity, AI systems can alert banks and customers to potential threats much more quickly than traditional methods.

Retail: Personalization and Enhanced Customer Experience

In retail, AI personalizes the shopping experience like never before. Online retailers use AI to analyze browsing and purchase history to recommend products tailored to individual preferences. In physical stores, AI-driven tools help manage inventory and optimize store layouts based on customer behavior patterns.

Furthermore, AI enhances customer service through chatbots that provide instant, 24/7 assistance. These bots handle a range of queries, from tracking orders to resolving common issues, improving customer experience and efficiency.

Agriculture: Increasing Yield and Sustainability

AI in agriculture is increasing yield and promoting sustainability. Through precision farming, AI-driven systems analyze data from various sources, including satellites and sensors in the field, to provide farmers with detailed insights into crop health, soil conditions, and weather patterns. This information enables farmers to make better decisions about planting, irrigation, and harvesting, leading to increased crop yields and more sustainable practices.

Transportation: The Path Towards Autonomous Vehicles

The transportation industry is on the cusp of a revolution with the development of autonomous vehicles (AVs). AI algorithms process data from sensors and cameras to navigate roads, recognize obstacles, and make split-second decisions. While fully autonomous vehicles are still in development, the technology promises to improve road safety, reduce traffic congestion, and transform urban transportation.

Energy: Efficient Management and Renewable Integration

AI is making energy systems more efficient and aiding the integration of renewable sources. AI-driven grid management systems analyze data to predict energy demand, optimize distribution, and reduce waste. In renewable energy, AI optimizes the operation of wind and solar farms, predicting weather patterns and adjusting turbines and panels to maximize energy capture.

Challenges and Ethical Considerations

As AI transforms industries, it also brings challenges and ethical considerations. The displacement of jobs by automation, the need for new skill sets, data privacy, and the risk of algorithmic bias are issues that need addressing. Ensuring ethical use of AI and preparing the workforce for an AI-driven economy are paramount for sustainable growth.

AI's impact on industries is profound and widespread, offering opportunities for increased efficiency, innovation, and sustainability. From manufacturing to healthcare, finance to agriculture, AI is not just reshaping business models; it's redefining the boundaries of what's possible. As we move forward, the key to harnessing AI's full potential lies in balancing technological advancement with responsible and ethical practices.

AI in Marketing and Customer Experience

In the dynamic world of marketing, Artificial Intelligence (AI) is a game-changer, redefining how brands interact with customers and shaping the overall customer experience. The integration of AI in marketing strategies and customer service is not just a trend but a fundamental shift towards more personalized, efficient, and insightful consumer engagement.

Personalization at Scale

Customized Consumer Interactions: AI excels in personalizing marketing efforts. By analyzing customer data – including browsing habits, purchase history, and preferences – AI algorithms can tailor product recommendations, marketing messages, and promotions to individual consumers. This level of personalization increases customer engagement and satisfaction, leading to higher conversion rates and loyalty.

Dynamic Content Optimization: AI systems dynamically adjust website content, emails, and advertisements to suit individual user profiles. This real-time customization ensures that consumers are presented with the most relevant and appealing content, enhancing the effectiveness of marketing campaigns.

Enhancing Customer Experience through AI-driven Insights

Predictive Analytics: AI's predictive analytics capabilities enable businesses to anticipate customer needs and preferences, even before the customer realizes them. By analyzing patterns and trends, AI can predict future buying behaviors, helping businesses stay ahead of the curve in meeting customer expectations.

Sentiment Analysis: Through sentiment analysis, AI tools assess customer feedback, reviews, and social media conversations to gauge public sentiment about a brand or product. This insight is invaluable for adjusting marketing strategies, addressing customer concerns, and improving product offerings.

Chatbots and Virtual Assistants

24/7 Customer Service: AI-powered chatbots and virtual assistants provide round-the-clock customer support. Capable of handling a wide range of queries from basic information requests to complex problem-solving, these AI agents enhance customer support efficiency and response times.

Human-like Interaction: Advances in Natural Language Processing (NLP) enable these AI systems to interact in a more human-like manner, understanding and responding to customers' queries with increasing accuracy and context-awareness.

Targeted Advertising and Marketing Automation

Data-driven Targeting: AI algorithms analyze vast datasets to identify potential customers and target them with specific advertising campaigns. This data-driven approach ensures that marketing efforts are more focused and cost-effective.

Marketing Automation: From email marketing campaigns to social media posts, AI automates routine marketing tasks, freeing up human marketers to focus on more strategic and creative aspects of their work.

Customer Journey Mapping and Experience Optimization

Mapping the Customer Journey: AI tools map out the customer journey, identifying key touchpoints and interactions. This mapping helps businesses understand the customer's path to purchase and optimize their marketing strategies accordingly.

Experience Optimization: By continuously analyzing customer interaction data, AI identifies areas for improvement in the customer journey. This ongoing optimization process ensures a seamless and satisfying customer experience.

Ethical and Privacy Considerations

The use of AI in marketing and customer experience raises important questions about consumer privacy and data ethics. Businesses must navigate the delicate balance between personalization and privacy, ensuring that customer data is used responsibly and transparently.

Challenges and Future Directions

Overcoming AI Implementation Challenges: Implementing AI in marketing requires not only technological infrastructure but also a cultural shift within organizations. Businesses must embrace data-driven decision-making and foster skills necessary to leverage AI effectively.

Evolving Consumer Expectations: As consumers become more accustomed to personalized experiences, their expectations evolve. Businesses must continually adapt and innovate to meet these changing demands.

Future of AI in Marketing: The future of AI in marketing points towards more sophisticated personalization, predictive models, and automated content creation. The integration of AI with emerging technologies like augmented reality (AR) and virtual reality (VR) is set to create even more immersive and engaging marketing experiences.

AI has fundamentally transformed marketing and customer experience, offering unprecedented opportunities for personalization, efficiency, and insights. While it presents challenges, particularly in data ethics and implementation, its potential benefits are immense. As businesses continue to harness the power of AI, they will be better equipped to meet the evolving demands of consumers, creating more meaningful and rewarding customer relationships.

The Future of Work: AI and Automation

In this critical exploration, we delve into the profound implications of Artificial Intelligence (AI) and automation on the future of work. As AI systems become increasingly sophisticated, they're not only augmenting human capabilities but also reshaping the very nature of work itself. This evolution is sparking a major transformation in the global job market and workforce dynamics.

The convergence of AI and automation heralds a new age where routine tasks are increasingly performed by machines, freeing human talent for more creative and strategic roles. This shift, however, is a double-edged sword. While it promises increased efficiency and the birth of new professions, it also poses significant challenges, such as job displacement and the need for substantial reskilling of the workforce.

Industries ranging from manufacturing to services are witnessing a radical change in job roles and skills requirements. The automation of repetitive tasks is not just altering what work is done, but also how and by whom it is performed. As we stand at the brink of this transformation, it's crucial to navigate these changes thoughtfully, ensuring that the integration of AI and automation into the workplace leads to enhanced productivity, job creation, and a balanced evolution of the labor market.

Chapter 4
Ethical Considerations and AI

In Chapter 4, we delve into the intricate web of ethical considerations surrounding Artificial Intelligence (AI). As AI continues to advance and permeate every facet of our lives, it brings with it a host of ethical dilemmas and moral questions that challenge our traditional understanding of responsibility, privacy, and fairness. This chapter explores the complex ethical landscape that emerges from the intersection of AI with human values and societal norms.

The ethical implications of AI are as vast and varied as its applications. From data privacy and security concerns to the potential for bias and discrimination in AI algorithms, the ethical challenges are numerous and multifaceted. The advent of AI has also sparked a debate on the extent to which we should allow these systems to make decisions that affect human lives, especially in critical areas like healthcare, law enforcement, and the military.

Furthermore, as AI systems become more autonomous, questions about accountability and transparency become increasingly pertinent. Who is responsible when an AI system makes a flawed decision? How can we ensure that AI systems are transparent and their decision-making processes understandable to humans?

This chapter aims to unravel these ethical quandaries, offering insights into how we might navigate this new terrain responsibly, ensuring that AI is developed and used in a manner that benefits society while upholding our ethical principles.

The Ethics of AI: Privacy, Bias, and Control

Artificial Intelligence (AI) has the potential to profoundly impact society, but with this potential comes a range of ethical considerations, particularly around privacy, bias, and control. This detailed discussion examines these ethical challenges, exploring how they manifest in real-world AI applications and the measures needed to address them.

Privacy in the Age of AI

AI's ability to process vast amounts of data is one of its greatest strengths, but it also poses significant privacy concerns.

Data Collection and Surveillance: AI systems often require large datasets to learn and make decisions. The collection of such data, especially personal data, raises concerns over surveillance and the erosion of privacy. Facial recognition technology, for instance, can be used for beneficial purposes like finding missing persons but also for mass surveillance.

Data Security and Consent: Ensuring the security of data used by AI systems and obtaining consent for its use are critical. Data breaches can expose sensitive personal information, and there's the question of whether individuals are adequately informed and consenting to how their data is used.

Informational Self-Determination: This concept revolves around an individual's right to control their personal data. AI challenges this right, as individuals may not know what data is collected, how it's analyzed, or for what purposes it's used.

Bias in AI Systems

AI systems are only as unbiased as the data they are trained on and the designers who create them.

Algorithmic Bias: When AI algorithms are trained on biased data, they can perpetuate and amplify existing prejudices. This is evident in areas like hiring, where AI recruitment tools might show bias against certain demographic groups.

Mitigating Bias: Addressing this requires a conscious effort to use diverse training datasets and involve diverse teams in AI development. It also involves continuous monitoring for biased outcomes and adjusting algorithms accordingly.

Transparency and Accountability: There's a need for transparency in how AI systems make decisions, especially when these decisions impact people's lives. Understanding an AI's decision-making process is key to identifying and correcting bias.

Control and Autonomy

The increasing sophistication of AI systems raises questions about control and human autonomy.

Decision-making Authority: As AI systems become more capable, there's a temptation to delegate more decision-making to them, from everyday choices like movie recommendations to significant decisions in healthcare or criminal justice. This delegation raises concerns about the loss of human oversight and autonomy.

Autonomous Systems and Lethal AI: The use of AI in autonomous weapons systems is particularly contentious. The idea of machines making life-and-death decisions without human intervention brings ethical, moral, and legal questions to the forefront.

Regulating AI Autonomy: To address these concerns, there's a growing call for regulation and guidelines around the development and use of autonomous AI systems. Ensuring that these systems are designed with safeguards to prevent unintended harm and that there's always a way for human intervention is critical.

Ethical Frameworks and Policies

Developing and implementing ethical frameworks and policies is essential in guiding the responsible development and use of AI.

Ethical Guidelines for AI: Many organizations and governments are proposing ethical guidelines for AI, emphasizing principles like transparency, fairness, and accountability.

Legislation and Regulation: Alongside ethical guidelines, there's a need for robust legislation and regulation to ensure that AI is used in a way that aligns with societal values and protects individuals' rights.

Global Collaboration: Given the global nature of AI and technology, international collaboration is crucial in developing standards and norms for ethical AI.

The ethical implications of AI in areas like privacy, bias, and control are profound and complex. Addressing these issues is not just a technical challenge but a societal one, requiring a multidisciplinary approach that includes technologists, ethicists, policymakers, and the public. As AI continues to evolve, it is crucial that ethical considerations are at the forefront of its development and deployment, ensuring that AI serves humanity positively and responsibly.

AI Governance and Policy Making

The burgeoning growth of Artificial Intelligence (AI) necessitates robust governance and policy-making to ensure its ethical, responsible, and beneficial use. AI governance involves setting guidelines and frameworks that direct the development and application of AI technologies. This in-depth discussion explores the critical elements of AI governance and the intricacies of policy-making in this dynamic field.

The Need for AI Governance

As AI technologies increasingly influence various sectors, the need for governance frameworks becomes paramount. Effective governance ensures that AI advances in a way that aligns with societal values and ethical principles, mitigating risks while maximizing benefits.

Risk Management: AI poses unique risks, including biases in decision-making, infringement of privacy, and potential misuse. Governance frameworks aim to identify, assess, and manage these risks.

Ethical Guidelines: Establishing ethical guidelines for AI development and use ensures respect for human rights, fairness, transparency, and accountability.

Public Trust: Robust governance fosters public trust in AI technologies. Clear regulations and ethical standards reassure the public that AI systems are safe, reliable, and aligned with the public interest.

Frameworks for AI Policy Making

AI policy-making involves developing regulations and standards that guide AI's development and deployment.

National and International Policies: Countries worldwide are developing national AI strategies. International bodies like the EU, UNESCO, and OECD are also proposing frameworks for AI governance, emphasizing global collaboration.

Regulatory Balance: Policymaking must strike a balance between fostering innovation and addressing ethical, social, and economic concerns. Overregulation may hinder technological advancement, while underregulation could lead to unintended consequences.

Sector-specific Policies: Different sectors may require tailored AI governance strategies. For instance, AI in healthcare demands stringent privacy protections, whereas AI in autonomous vehicles requires safety and liability regulations.

Transparency and Accountability in AI Systems

Transparent AI systems enable users to understand and trust AI decision-making processes.

Explainable AI: Developing AI systems that provide explanations for their decisions and actions is crucial, especially in high-stakes domains like healthcare and criminal justice.

Accountability Mechanisms: Assigning accountability for AI decisions can be challenging, particularly with complex and autonomous systems. Policymaking must establish who is responsible for AI decisions and actions—be it developers, users, or manufacturers.

Data Privacy and Security

The vast amount of data used by AI systems raises significant privacy and security concerns.

Data Protection Regulations: Policies like the General Data Protection Regulation (GDPR) provide a framework for data privacy and user rights regarding personal data. Similar regulations worldwide govern how AI can use personal data.

Data Governance: Data governance policies ensure the integrity, security, and ethical use of data in AI systems, protecting against breaches and misuse.

Human-centric AI Development

AI governance should prioritize human welfare and societal well-being.

Inclusive and Fair AI: Policies must ensure AI systems do not perpetuate discrimination or bias, promoting inclusivity and fairness in AI applications.

AI for Social Good: Encouraging the use of AI in solving societal challenges, like climate change and healthcare, can maximize its positive impact.

Stakeholder Engagement and Multidisciplinary Approach

AI governance requires the involvement of various stakeholders, including governments, industry, academia, and civil society.

Collaborative Policymaking: Involving a range of stakeholders in AI policy discussions ensures diverse perspectives and needs are considered.

Research and Education: Supporting AI research and promoting education in AI ethics and policy can build a knowledgeable base for effective governance.

Challenges in AI Governance

AI governance faces several challenges, including the fast pace of AI development, international coordination, and the need for flexibility in regulatory approaches to accommodate emerging technologies.

Future Directions in AI Governance

Looking ahead, AI governance and policy-making will need to evolve continuously to keep pace with technological advancements. This includes adopting adaptive regulatory approaches and fostering international cooperation to address the global nature of AI challenges.

Effective governance and policy-making are crucial in navigating the complex landscape of AI. They provide the necessary frameworks to ensure AI's development and use are ethical, secure, and beneficial for society. As AI continues to evolve, ongoing efforts in governance and policy-making will play a pivotal role in shaping its future and ensuring it serves the greater good.

Chapter 5

AI and the Global Society

Chapter 5 of "Echoes of Tomorrow: AI and the Future of Society" turns the lens towards the global impact of Artificial Intelligence (AI). This ubiquitous technology, transcending borders and cultures, holds the power to transform societies around the world. From the bustling metropolises of the developed world to the rural landscapes of developing nations, AI's influence is both vast and varied, promising opportunities while also posing unique challenges

In this chapter, we explore how AI is reshaping the global landscape, influencing economies, and altering social dynamics. We examine its role in bridging or, conversely, widening the gap between different regions and socio-economic strata. The focus extends to how AI is addressing global challenges like healthcare accessibility, environmental sustainability, and education, highlighting its potential as a force for good.

Simultaneously, we confront the stark realities of this technological proliferation, including the risks of widening inequality, the digital divide, and the geopolitical implications of AI leadership. This global perspective on AI is crucial in understanding its multifaceted impact on human society and in charting a course towards a future where its benefits are equitably shared, and its challenges are collectively addressed.

AI in Developing Countries

The advent of Artificial Intelligence (AI) presents unique opportunities and challenges for developing countries. While AI has the potential to drive growth, improve services, and address socio-economic issues, it also poses risks of exacerbating inequalities and creating new divides. This comprehensive discussion examines the multifaceted impact of AI in developing nations.

Opportunities Presented by AI

Healthcare Advancements: AI can revolutionize healthcare in developing countries by improving diagnostics, disease prediction, and treatment accessibility. AI-driven tools can help overcome shortages of medical professionals by offering remote consultation and diagnostic services, and by aiding in the interpretation of medical images and data, especially in remote or underserved areas.

Agricultural Improvements: AI technologies can significantly enhance agricultural practices, crucial in countries where agriculture is a major economic sector. AI can provide insights for precision farming, pest control, crop disease detection, and yield optimization, thus boosting productivity and sustainability.

Education and Skill Development: AI can play a pivotal role in bridging educational gaps. Through personalized learning tools and online education platforms, AI can provide access to quality education resources, catering to diverse learning needs and overcoming geographical and socio-economic barriers.

Financial Inclusion: AI-driven solutions in fintech are aiding financial inclusion, offering services like credit scoring, mobile banking, and personalized financial advice. This is particularly important in regions where a large segment of the population is unbanked or underbanked.

Challenges and Risks

Digital Divide: One of the major challenges in harnessing AI in developing countries is the digital divide. Limited access to technology, lack of infrastructure, and low internet penetration can hinder the effective implementation of AI solutions.

AI and Employment Concerns: There are concerns that AI and automation could lead to job displacement, especially in sectors that heavily rely on unskilled labor. Developing strategies for workforce reskilling and embracing AI technologies that create new job opportunities are crucial.

Data Privacy and Security: Developing countries often lack stringent data protection laws and enforcement mechanisms. This raises concerns about data privacy and security, especially as AI systems require vast amounts of data to function effectively.

AI Governance and Ethical Use: Establishing robust frameworks for AI governance and ensuring ethical use are challenging in developing countries due to limited resources and expertise in this field.

Strategies for Maximizing AI Benefits

Investing in Infrastructure and Connectivity: To fully leverage AI, it is vital for developing countries to invest in digital infrastructure, including internet connectivity, data centers, and technological literacy programs.

Fostering Local AI Ecosystems: Developing local AI ecosystems through education, training, and research can help tailor AI solutions to specific regional needs and challenges.

Public-Private Partnerships: Collaborations between governments, private sector, and international organizations can accelerate AI adoption and ensure it addresses key development challenges.

Policy and Regulatory Frameworks: Implementing policies and regulations that foster innovation while protecting citizens' rights and promoting ethical AI use is essential.

Focusing on Sustainable AI Applications: Prioritizing AI applications in areas such as environmental conservation, healthcare, and education can drive sustainable development.

The Role of International Cooperation

International cooperation can play a significant role in supporting AI initiatives in developing countries. Sharing knowledge, resources, and best practices can help overcome technological and infrastructural barriers.

Real-World Examples of AI in Developing Countries

AI for Disease Control: AI applications in disease surveillance and control, such as predicting outbreaks and optimizing resource allocation for disease prevention, have shown promising results in several developing nations.

AI in Agriculture: Projects using AI for predicting weather patterns, soil health analysis, and crop monitoring are helping farmers in developing countries increase yields and reduce losses.

Educational AI Tools: AI-powered educational platforms are being used to provide personalized learning experiences in regions with limited access to quality education.

AI presents a remarkable opportunity for developing countries to leapfrog traditional stages of development and address longstanding challenges. However, realizing this potential requires concerted efforts in infrastructure development, policy-making, education, and ethical governance. Balancing the benefits and risks of AI, and ensuring it serves the broader goals of sustainable development and social equity, is key to harnessing its power for positive change in these nations.

The Role of AI in Environmental Sustainability

As the world grapples with escalating environmental challenges, Artificial Intelligence (AI) emerges as a powerful tool for driving sustainability. This comprehensive analysis explores how AI contributes to environmental protection and resource conservation, offering innovative solutions to some of the most pressing ecological issues.

Climate Change and Emission Reduction

Predictive Analysis for Climate Modeling: AI significantly enhances climate modeling and forecasting. By processing vast amounts of environmental data, AI algorithms can predict climate trends, model potential scenarios, and inform policy decisions on climate change mitigation.

Optimizing Energy Consumption: AI systems are instrumental in optimizing energy use in various sectors, from industrial processes to residential homes. Smart grids, powered by AI, balance energy supply and demand more efficiently, integrating renewable energy sources effectively and reducing overall emissions.

Emission Control in Industries: AI applications in industries monitor and manage emissions, identify inefficiencies, and recommend improvements to reduce the carbon footprint. In automotive, AI is pivotal in advancing electric vehicle technology and optimizing fuel efficiency in traditional vehicles.

Biodiversity and Ecosystem Preservation

Wildlife Monitoring and Conservation: AI-driven technologies, like camera traps and acoustic sensors, monitor wildlife populations and habitats. Machine learning algorithms analyze this data to track animal movements, detect poaching activities, and inform conservation strategies.

Forest Management: AI helps in forest management by analyzing satellite images to detect deforestation, forest degradation, and illegal logging activities. This real-time monitoring enables swift action to protect these critical ecosystems.

Marine Conservation: In marine environments, AI tools analyze data from satellites and underwater sensors to monitor ocean health, track marine species, and manage fisheries sustainably.

Sustainable Agriculture and Water Management

Precision Agriculture: AI transforms agricultural practices by enabling precision farming. It analyzes data from various sources to guide farmers on crop rotation, soil health, water usage, and pest control, leading to higher crop yields with reduced environmental impact.

Water Resource Management: AI systems analyze patterns in water usage and predict future water needs. They play a crucial role in managing water resources efficiently, detecting leaks, and ensuring sustainable water supply in areas facing water scarcity.

Waste Management and Recycling

Efficient Waste Sorting: AI-powered robots and sorting systems enhance waste management by accurately sorting recyclable materials, reducing contamination, and improving recycling rates.

Waste Reduction Strategies: AI algorithms analyze consumption patterns and waste generation, aiding businesses and cities in developing strategies to minimize waste and promote a circular economy.

Renewable Energy Advancements

Optimizing Renewable Energy Production: AI is key in optimizing the operation of renewable energy sources like wind and solar. It predicts energy generation patterns, adjusts to changing weather conditions, and integrates renewable energy smoothly into the power grid.

Energy Storage and Distribution: AI aids in managing energy storage systems, ensuring that excess energy generated from renewable sources is stored efficiently and distributed based on demand.

Challenges and Ethical Considerations

While AI offers promising solutions for environmental sustainability, it also presents challenges and ethical considerations:

Energy Consumption of AI Systems: Large AI models require significant computational power, leading to high energy consumption. Ensuring that the energy used for these systems is sourced sustainably is crucial.

Data Privacy and Security: The vast amounts of data collected for environmental monitoring raise concerns about privacy and security, necessitating stringent data protection measures.

Inclusivity and Accessibility: It is essential that AI-driven environmental solutions are accessible to all regions, including those with limited technological infrastructure.

AI stands as a beacon of hope in the quest for environmental sustainability. Its applications in climate change mitigation, ecosystem preservation, sustainable agriculture, water management, waste reduction, and renewable energy are paving the way for a more sustainable and resilient future. However, harnessing AI's potential for environmental good requires a balanced approach, considering its energy demands, ethical implications, and the need for inclusive access. As we continue to innovate, the thoughtful and responsible application of AI in environmental sustainability efforts could prove pivotal in preserving our planet for future generations.

Chapter 6

The Future of AI Technology

Chapter 6 peers into the horizon of Artificial Intelligence (AI) to explore the tantalizing possibilities and forthcoming advancements in this rapidly evolving field. As we stand at the cusp of what many consider a golden age of AI, it's crucial to envision and understand what the future may hold. This chapter ventures into the realms of emerging AI technologies, contemplating their potential impacts and the new challenges they may bring.

We delve into the realms of advanced machine learning, deep learning, quantum computing, and how these are set to further revolutionize AI capabilities. We'll examine the strides towards achieving Artificial General Intelligence (AGI), an AI with the ability to understand, learn, and apply its intelligence to a wide array of problems, much like a human brain. This journey also takes us through the ethical, societal, and technical challenges that accompany these advancements.

The chapter discusses the integration of AI in various domains – from personal computing to industrial applications – predicting how these technologies will shape our future lifestyles, economies, and work environments. We also ponder the implications of such advancements for global policy, governance, and the human-AI relationship.

Emerging Trends in AI Research

As we progress deeper into the 21st century, Artificial Intelligence (AI) research is rapidly evolving, continuously pushing the boundaries of what's possible. This comprehensive analysis delves into the current emerging trends in AI research, offering a glimpse into the future of this transformative technology.

Towards Artificial General Intelligence (AGI)

One of the most ambitious goals in AI research is achieving Artificial General Intelligence (AGI) – AI that can understand, learn, and apply its intelligence across a wide range of tasks, much like a human. Unlike current AI, which excels in specific tasks (narrow AI), AGI would possess holistic understanding and cognitive capabilities. Researchers are exploring new models and algorithms to create more adaptable and generalizable AI systems, though AGI remains a long-term goal.

Quantum Computing and AI

The integration of quantum computing and AI is a burgeoning area of research. Quantum computers, with their ability to perform complex calculations at unprecedented speeds, could unlock new possibilities for AI. They could significantly enhance machine learning algorithms, optimize AI decision-making processes, and solve complex optimization problems that are currently intractable for traditional computers.

Explainable AI (XAI)

As AI systems become more prevalent, the demand for transparency and understanding of their decision-making processes grows. Explainable AI focuses on creating AI models that are transparent and their workings understandable to humans. This trend is crucial for critical applications like healthcare, finance, and law, where understanding AI's rationale is as important as the decision itself.

AI for Environmental Sustainability

AI research is increasingly focusing on addressing global environmental challenges. This includes using AI for climate modeling, pollution control, renewable energy optimization, and biodiversity conservation. AI is being employed to analyze environmental data, predict ecological trends, and propose sustainable solutions.

5. Ethical AI and Algorithmic Fairness

With growing awareness of AI's societal impact, there's an increased focus on ethical AI and algorithmic fairness. This research trend involves developing AI systems that are unbiased, fair, and do not perpetuate existing societal inequalities. Efforts are underway to create algorithms that are transparent and accountable, with built-in checks for bias and discrimination.

AI in Healthcare: Beyond Diagnosis

While AI's role in diagnostics is well-established, emerging research is exploring its potential in personalized treatment plans, drug development, and mental health. AI algorithms are being developed to analyze patient history, lifestyle, and genetic information to recommend customized treatment plans, offering a more personalized approach to healthcare.

Neuro-Symbolic AI

This emerging field combines neural networks (used in deep learning) with symbolic AI (based on human-readable symbols and logic). Neuro-symbolic AI aims to create more versatile and robust AI systems that can learn from data (like neural networks) while also understanding and manipulating abstract concepts (like symbolic AI). This approach could lead to AI systems with improved reasoning capabilities and common-sense understanding.

AI-Enabled Robotics

Advancements in AI are significantly enhancing the capabilities of robots. Research is focused on developing robots that can learn from their environment, adapt to new tasks, and interact more naturally with humans. This includes advancements in areas like reinforcement learning, human-robot interaction, and robotic manipulation.

AI in Edge Computing

Edge AI involves processing AI algorithms locally, on the device, rather than in a centralized cloud-based system. This trend is particularly relevant for applications requiring real-time processing, like autonomous vehicles and IoT devices. Edge AI research is focused on optimizing AI algorithms to run efficiently on less powerful devices.

Augmented Creativity

AI is not just automating tasks; it's enhancing human creativity. AI algorithms are being developed to assist in creative processes like design, art, music, and literature. This research explores the collaboration between human and AI creativity, leading to novel forms of artistic expression and design innovation.

The current trends in AI research are diverse and dynamic, reflecting the technology's broad impact across various domains. From striving for AGI to ensuring ethical and sustainable use of AI, the research landscape is as challenging as it is promising. As these trends continue to evolve, they will undoubtedly shape the future trajectory of AI, heralding a new era of innovation and societal transformation.

Potential Breakthroughs and Their Implications

The field of Artificial Intelligence (AI) is ripe for breakthroughs that could significantly alter technology, society, and our daily lives. This detailed exploration delves into several potential AI breakthroughs and their far-reaching implications.

Achieving True Artificial General Intelligence (AGI)

The quest for AGI – an AI system with the ability to understand, learn, and apply its intelligence across a diverse range of tasks – remains the holy grail of AI research. A breakthrough in AGI would signify the development of AI systems with cognitive abilities akin to human intellect, capable of reasoning, problem-solving, and creative thinking across various domains.

Implications: AGI would revolutionize numerous fields, from scientific research to complex decision-making. It could lead to major advancements in medical research, climate modeling, and space exploration. However, it also raises ethical and safety concerns, including issues of control, the impact on employment, and the need for robust regulatory frameworks.

Quantum AI

Combining quantum computing with AI could lead to exponential increases in computational power. Quantum AI could solve problems intractable for classical computers, such as simulating molecular interactions for drug discovery or optimizing large, complex systems.

Implications: Quantum AI could drastically reduce the time and cost for new drug development, revolutionize materials science, and provide solutions to optimize supply chains and traffic systems. However, it may also create challenges in cybersecurity and require new paradigms in programming and algorithm design.

Explainable AI (XAI) Becoming Normative

Current AI systems often operate as 'black boxes', offering little insight into how they reach conclusions. A breakthrough in XAI would make AI decisions transparent, understandable, and trustable, especially in critical sectors like healthcare and justice.

Implications: XAI would enhance trust and adoption of AI in sensitive areas, improve regulatory compliance, and facilitate correction of biases in AI models. It would also empower end-users and policymakers to understand and appropriately trust AI solutions.

4. Personalized AI Assistants Evolving into Digital Twins

The evolution of personalized AI assistants into 'digital twins'—highly personalized AI models that understand individual preferences, habits, and needs—is another potential breakthrough. These AI systems could act as personal advisors, healthcare monitors, and efficiency enhancers.

Implications: Digital twins could revolutionize personal productivity, healthcare (through personalized monitoring and advice), and even social interactions. Privacy and security concerns would be paramount, as such systems would require access to extensive personal data.

5. AI in Climate Change Mitigation

AI has the potential to significantly contribute to combating climate change. Breakthroughs in this area could involve advanced modeling of climate systems, optimization of renewable energy resources, and development of carbon capture technologies.

Implications: Efficiently addressing climate change, managing renewable energy, and predicting environmental changes would have profound global impacts. However, this requires global collaboration and data sharing, posing geopolitical and ethical challenges.

6. Neuromorphic Computing and AI

Neuromorphic computing, which involves designing computer hardware to mimic the human brain's structures and processes, could revolutionize AI's efficiency and capabilities. This breakthrough would allow AI systems to process information more like a human brain, leading to more efficient and powerful AI models.

Implications: Neuromorphic computing could lead to AI systems that are more adaptable, require less energy, and can make decisions more efficiently. It would have significant impacts on robotics, edge computing, and IoT devices.

Autonomous Systems in Complex Environments

Significant advancements in autonomous systems, enabling operation in complex, unstructured environments, would be a major breakthrough. This includes fully autonomous vehicles in urban settings, drones for delivery and monitoring, and robots capable of performing complex tasks in dynamic environments.

Implications: The widespread deployment of autonomous systems could transform urban mobility, logistics, and service industries, but also raise issues around safety, ethics, and employment.

These potential AI breakthroughs present a landscape brimming with transformative possibilities. However, they also bring to the fore critical implications for society, economy, and ethical norms. Balancing the benefits of these advancements with their potential risks will be a key challenge, requiring proactive policy making, international cooperation, and a multidisciplinary approach to ensure they contribute positively to society.

Chapter 7

Preparing for an AI Future

In Chapter 7, "Preparing for an AI Future," we address the pivotal question: how do we ready ourselves for a world increasingly shaped by Artificial Intelligence? This chapter is dedicated to understanding the shifts needed in education, workforce, policy-making, and societal attitudes to adapt to an AI-driven future. It is a guide to embracing the opportunities and mitigating the challenges presented by the advance of AI.

We explore the evolving landscape of education and training, emphasizing the need to cultivate AI literacy and adapt curricular offerings to prepare new generations for AI-augmented workplaces. This discussion extends to the workforce, where continuous learning and reskilling become essential in a landscape where many traditional jobs are transformed or replaced by AI.

Further, we delve into the critical role of policy-makers in shaping a future where AI is used ethically and beneficially. This involves creating robust legal frameworks, ethical guidelines, and ensuring that AI advancements are aligned with societal values and needs.

Lastly, this chapter discusses how society as a whole can adapt to an AI future. It addresses the importance of public awareness and engagement with AI, fostering a culture that views AI as a collaborative tool for enhancing human capabilities rather than a replacement for them.

Education and Skill Development for an AI Era

In an era increasingly influenced by Artificial Intelligence (AI), education and skill development must adapt to prepare individuals for a rapidly changing landscape. This comprehensive discussion explores the essential facets of education and training in the context of an AI-driven future.

Building AI Literacy

The first step in adapting education for an AI era is fostering AI literacy across all levels of society. This involves:

Basic Understanding of AI: Introducing AI concepts in school curricula, not limited to computer science but across subjects, to provide a foundational understanding of AI technologies and their applications.

Awareness of AI Implications: Educating students about the ethical, social, and economic implications of AI. This includes discussions on privacy, job displacement, and the societal impact of automation.

Specialized AI Training

For those pursuing specialized careers in AI, advanced education and training are crucial:

Advanced Degree Programs: Universities should offer specialized programs in AI, machine learning, data science, and robotics. These programs must be regularly updated to reflect the latest advancements in the field.

Industry-Specific AI Skills: As AI permeates various industries, specialized training programs tailored to specific sectors (like healthcare, finance, or manufacturing) are essential.

Emphasis on Soft Skills

With AI automating many technical and analytical tasks, soft skills become more important:

Problem Solving and Critical Thinking: Training in critical thinking and complex problem-solving to work alongside AI systems.

Creativity and Innovation: Encouraging creativity and innovation in education to ensure that humans continue to lead in ideation and design, areas where AI still lags behind.

Emotional Intelligence: Strengthening emotional intelligence skills, crucial for roles that require empathy, understanding, and interpersonal communication.

Lifelong Learning and Reskilling

The evolving nature of AI technology necessitates continuous learning:

Reskilling Programs: Development of reskilling programs for professionals impacted by AI and automation. These should be accessible and flexible to accommodate diverse learning paces and styles.

Online Learning and Certifications: Leveraging online platforms for ongoing education and certification in AI-related fields, making lifelong learning more accessible.

Integrating Ethics into AI Education

Ethical considerations must be an integral part of AI education:

Ethics in AI Design and Use: Teaching ethical design and deployment of AI systems to prevent biases and ensure fair and responsible use.

Policy and Governance: Education on AI policy and governance to prepare future leaders for decision-making roles in an AI-influenced world.

Promoting Collaboration Skills

With AI teams often being interdisciplinary, collaboration skills are crucial:

Interdisciplinary Teamwork: Training in working effectively in interdisciplinary teams, combining AI expertise with domain-specific knowledge.

Human-AI Collaboration: Understanding how to collaborate with AI systems in problem-solving and decision-making processes.

Fostering an Interdisciplinary Approach

AI's impact spans multiple domains, making an interdisciplinary approach vital:

Combining AI with Other Disciplines: Integrating AI education with other fields like environmental science, public policy, or healthcare.

Project-Based Learning: Implementing project-based learning that allows students to apply AI in real-world interdisciplinary scenarios.

Developing a Global Perspective

AI education should incorporate a global perspective:

Cultural Sensitivity and Bias Awareness: Educating about cultural differences and the importance of developing AI systems that are globally inclusive and unbiased.

International Collaboration: Encouraging international collaboration in AI research and education to address global challenges.

Preparing for an AI-driven future requires a multifaceted approach to education and skill development. It involves not only technical training but also the cultivation of soft skills, ethical understanding, and a lifelong learning mindset. Educators, policymakers, and industry leaders must work together to design educational frameworks that equip individuals with the skills needed to navigate, contribute to, and thrive in an AI-augmented world. This approach will ensure that the workforce is not only capable of using AI effectively but also of steering its development in ethical, socially beneficial directions.

Shaping Policies for an AI-Driven World

In an increasingly AI-driven world, shaping effective policies is crucial for harnessing the benefits of Artificial Intelligence (AI) while mitigating its risks. This comprehensive discussion focuses on the key aspects of policy-making in the context of AI's rapid advancement.

Establishing Ethical Guidelines for AI

Developing and enforcing ethical guidelines is a foundational step in AI policy-making.

Universal AI Ethics Standards: Policies should promote universal standards for AI ethics, focusing on transparency, accountability, fairness, and respect for privacy.

Mitigating Biases: Policies must address biases in AI algorithms and data, ensuring AI systems are equitable and do not perpetuate discrimination.

Privacy Protections: Legislations akin to the General Data Protection Regulation (GDPR) should be enacted globally, safeguarding personal data used by AI systems.

Fostering Innovation While Ensuring Safety

Balancing innovation and safety is key in AI policy-making.

Support for Research and Development: Governments should invest in AI research, providing grants and incentives for innovation while ensuring safety and ethical considerations are integral.

Regulations for High-Risk AI Applications: Specific regulations for high-risk applications, such as autonomous vehicles or healthcare diagnostics, are essential to ensure public safety.

Preparing the Workforce for AI Transformation

Addressing the workforce transformation due to AI is critical.

Reskilling and Upskilling Programs: Policymakers should facilitate reskilling programs for workers displaced by AI and promote upskilling opportunities to prepare the workforce for an AI-integrated job market.

Educational Reforms: Educational systems must be reformed to include AI literacy and skills relevant in an AI-driven economy, from primary education through higher education.

Promoting AI Accessibility and Inclusivity

Ensuring AI technology is accessible and inclusive is vital for equitable development.

Bridging the Digital Divide: Policies should aim to bridge the digital divide, ensuring all regions and communities have access to AI technology and its benefits.

Support for Diverse AI Development: Encouraging diversity in AI development teams can help create AI systems that are inclusive and sensitive to different cultures and needs.

International Collaboration and Standardization

AI's global nature necessitates international collaboration.

Harmonizing AI Regulations: International bodies should work towards harmonizing AI regulations to facilitate global cooperation and prevent regulatory conflicts.

Global Standards for AI: Developing global standards for AI interoperability, security, and ethics can facilitate international collaboration and trade in AI technologies.

Addressing the Societal Impact of AI

Policies must consider AI's broader societal impact.

Social Welfare Policies: As AI transforms industries, social welfare policies must evolve to address potential job displacement and ensure social safety nets.

Public Engagement and AI Education: Governments should engage the public in AI policy discussions and invest in public education about AI's benefits and challenges.

Regulating AI in Critical Sectors

Regulating AI in sectors such as healthcare, finance, and transportation is essential.

Sector-Specific Regulations: Detailed regulations tailored to specific sectors can address unique risks associated with AI applications in these areas.

Ethical Use in Critical Sectors: Policies should ensure AI is used ethically in critical sectors, prioritizing human welfare and safety.

Data Governance in an AI Context

Effective data governance is key for responsible AI development.

Data Privacy Laws: Strong data privacy laws are necessary to protect individuals' data used in AI systems.

Data Quality Standards: Setting standards for data quality and integrity can enhance AI systems' reliability and fairness.

Encouraging Ethical AI Entrepreneurship

Policies should encourage ethical AI entrepreneurship.

Incentives for Ethical AI Startups: Providing incentives for startups focusing on ethical AI development can promote responsible innovation.

Support for Small and Medium Enterprises (SMEs): SMEs should be supported in adopting AI technologies, ensuring they are not left behind in the AI revolution.

Preparing for AI-Induced Geopolitical Changes

AI induces significant geopolitical changes that need policy attention.

National Security Policies: National security policies must adapt to the challenges and opportunities posed by AI in defense and cybersecurity.

Global AI Leadership: Policies should aim at positioning countries as leaders in ethical, safe, and beneficial AI development and use.

Shaping policies for an AI-driven world requires a multi-faceted approach, addressing ethical guidelines, innovation, workforce transformation, inclusivity, international collaboration, societal impacts, sector-specific regulations, data governance, entrepreneurship, and geopolitical shifts. As AI continues to evolve, policy frameworks must be dynamic and adaptable, ensuring they keep pace with technological advancements while safeguarding societal values and well-being.

Chapter 8

Dystopia or Utopia? Contrasting Visions of AI's Impact

In a world progressively influenced by Artificial Intelligence (AI), the imperative to shape effective and forward-thinking policies has never been more critical. The ascendancy of AI presents unparalleled opportunities but also unprecedented challenges that cut across ethical, economic, social, and political realms. As we venture further into this AI-driven era, it becomes essential to formulate policies that not only harness AI's potential for innovation and advancement but also mitigate its risks and ensure equitable benefits for all.

This discourse begins by examining the necessity of establishing ethical frameworks and standards that govern AI development and application, ensuring that these advancements are aligned with societal values and human rights. It then navigates the complex interplay between fostering AI-driven innovation and safeguarding public safety, particularly in critical applications that significantly impact society. The transformation of the workforce in response to AI, a pivotal aspect of this era, demands a comprehensive strategy focusing on education, reskilling, and job creation.

Furthermore, the discourse delves into the need for global cooperation in AI governance, addressing not only the technological and economic aspects but also the broader implications on international relations and security. As we delve deeper into the nuances of AI policy-making, the goal remains clear: to steer the AI revolution towards a future that is not only technologically advanced but also ethically sound, socially responsible, and globally inclusive.

Optimistic Views on AI and Society

As we sail into the uncharted waters of the future, Artificial Intelligence (AI) stands as a beacon of hope and progress. Optimistic views on AI paint a picture of a world where this technology acts as a catalyst for positive societal transformation. Here is a detailed exploration of such perspectives.

Enhancing Human Capabilities

AI is seen as a powerful tool to augment human abilities rather than replace them.

Collaborative Intelligence: AI systems and humans can collaborate, combining the speed and efficiency of AI with the creativity and empathy of humans. This synergy could lead to unparalleled productivity and innovation.

Personal Assistants: AI-powered personal assistants could evolve to manage our schedules, optimize daily tasks, and even offer emotional support, leading to enhanced quality of life.

Revolutionizing Healthcare

The potential of AI in healthcare is enormous.

Accurate Diagnostics: AI's ability to analyze vast datasets can lead to more accurate diagnoses and early detection of diseases, significantly improving patient outcomes.

Personalized Treatment: AI's data-processing capabilities can tailor treatments to individual genetic profiles, ushering in a new era of personalized medicine.

Global Health Accessibility: AI can extend healthcare services to remote or underprivileged areas, bridging gaps in health accessibility.

Advancements in Education

AI could revolutionize education by personalizing learning experiences.

Customized Learning Paths: AI can adapt to individual learning styles, helping students grasp concepts at their own pace and style.

Accessibility in Learning: AI tools can make education more accessible to people with disabilities or those living in remote areas.

Sustainable Environmental Practices

AI has the potential to be a powerful ally in combating environmental challenges.

Climate Change Analysis: AI can process complex climate data to provide accurate predictions and effective strategies for combating climate change.

Resource Management: AI can optimize the use of natural resources, leading to more sustainable practices in agriculture, water management, and energy consumption.

Economic Growth and New Job Creation

Contrary to fears of job displacement, AI could spur economic growth and create new job categories.

New Industries and Roles: As AI evolves, new industries and roles will emerge, much like the internet era brought forth new career paths.

Enhanced Productivity: AI-driven automation can enhance productivity in various sectors, contributing to economic growth and development.

Improving Everyday Life

AI has the potential to greatly enhance daily living.

Smart Cities: AI can optimize traffic flow, enhance public safety, and improve utilities management in urban areas, making cities more livable and efficient.

Consumer Convenience: From smart homes to AI-driven recommendation systems, AI can add convenience and personalization to various aspects of consumer life.

Facilitating Scientific Discovery

AI could accelerate scientific discoveries.

Data Analysis: AI can analyze vast amounts of scientific data, identifying patterns and insights that might be missed by humans.

Drug Discovery: AI can speed up the process of drug discovery, reducing the time and cost to bring new treatments to market.

Strengthening Security

AI has significant applications in security.

Cybersecurity: AI can detect and respond to cybersecurity threats more rapidly and effectively than traditional methods.

Disaster Response: AI can assist in predicting and managing natural disasters, saving lives and resources.

Enhancing Global Connectivity

AI can contribute to a more connected world.

Language Translation: Advanced AI translation services can break down language barriers, fostering global communication and understanding.

Cultural Exchange: AI can facilitate cultural exchange by making global content more accessible across linguistic and geographical boundaries.

The optimistic view of AI in society is one of empowerment, enhancement, and enablement. This perspective envisions AI not as a threat but as a transformative force that, when guided by ethical principles and human-centric values, can lead to a more efficient, healthy, equitable, and interconnected world. As we continue to navigate the complexities of AI integration, maintaining this positive outlook, balanced with pragmatic caution, will be crucial for shaping a future where AI acts as a force for good.

Pessimistic Scenarios and Concerns

While the rise of Artificial Intelligence (AI) is often viewed with optimism, it is crucial to consider the potential pessimistic scenarios and concerns. These perspectives highlight the risks and challenges that could arise if AI development and deployment are not carefully managed.

Job Displacement and Economic Inequality

One of the most prominent concerns is the impact of AI on employment.

Automation of Jobs: AI and automation could lead to significant job displacement, especially in sectors like manufacturing, transportation, and customer service. This raises concerns about mass unemployment and the socio-economic consequences that could follow.

Widening Economic Divide: There's a risk that AI could exacerbate economic inequality. Those with AI skills or access to AI technology may prosper, while others could be left behind, deepening the divide between the "haves" and "have-nots."

Loss of Privacy and Surveillance

The pervasive use of AI in surveillance and data processing poses serious privacy concerns.

Invasive Surveillance: AI-powered surveillance systems could lead to a loss of privacy and freedom, with governments and corporations having the ability to monitor and analyze personal data on an unprecedented scale.

Data Misuse: The potential for misuse of personal data by AI systems, whether for commercial gain or more nefarious purposes, is a significant concern.

AI-Controlled Weaponry and Warfare

The militarization of AI technology presents alarming scenarios.

Autonomous Weapons: The development of autonomous weapons systems powered by AI raises ethical concerns about machines making life-and-death decisions, potentially leading to new forms of warfare.

Global Arms Race: An AI arms race could destabilize international relations, with nations competing to develop superior AI-powered weaponry.

Bias and Discrimination in AI Systems

The issue of bias in AI algorithms is a pressing concern.

Reinforcing Societal Biases: AI systems, if trained on biased data, could perpetuate and amplify existing societal biases, leading to discriminatory outcomes in areas like hiring, law enforcement, and credit scoring.

Lack of Diversity in AI Development: The underrepresentation of minority groups in AI development could lead to biased AI systems that do not adequately consider diverse perspectives and needs.

Dependence on AI and Loss of Human Skills

An over-reliance on AI could lead to the atrophy of certain human skills.

Erosion of Critical Thinking: As AI systems take over more decision-making tasks, there's a risk that human critical thinking and problem-solving skills could diminish.

Overdependence: Excessive reliance on AI for everyday tasks could lead to a scenario where humans are unable to function effectively without AI assistance.

AI Ethics and Governance Challenges

The rapid advancement of AI poses challenges in ethics and governance.

Regulatory Lag: The pace at which AI is advancing could outstrip the ability of governments and regulatory bodies to keep up, leading to a lack of adequate oversight and control.

Ethical Dilemmas: AI brings about ethical dilemmas that society may not be fully prepared to address, such as the moral implications of decision-making by AI systems.

Unintended Consequences and Catastrophic Scenarios

The complexity of AI systems raises concerns about unintended consequences.

Unpredictable Behavior: AI systems, especially those based on deep learning, can exhibit unpredictable behavior, leading to potentially dangerous outcomes.

Existential Risks: In extreme scenarios, superintelligent AI could pose existential risks to humanity if it develops in ways that are not aligned with human values and interests.

Socio-Cultural Impact

AI could also have profound impacts on society and culture.

Erosion of Human Interaction: The increasing use of AI in social contexts, such as companionship or care, could lead to a decline in human interactions and relationships.

Cultural Homogenization: AI-driven content recommendation systems could lead to cultural homogenization, where unique and diverse cultural expressions are undermined.

These pessimistic scenarios and concerns about AI are not inevitable outcomes but serve as crucial warnings. They highlight the need for responsible development and deployment of AI, emphasizing the importance of ethical considerations, robust governance, and proactive measures to mitigate potential negative impacts. By addressing these challenges head-on, society can steer AI development towards beneficial outcomes while safeguarding against its risks.

Chapter 9
AI in Art and Creativity

Chapter 9, "AI in Art and Creativity," opens a window into the captivating world where Artificial Intelligence (AI) intersects with human artistic expression. This exploration takes us into a realm where the lines between technology and art blur, revealing new forms of creativity that were once unimaginable. In this chapter, we delve into how AI is not just a tool or a medium, but a burgeoning collaborator in the arts, challenging our preconceptions about the nature of creativity and the essence of human expression.

From algorithmically generated paintings to AI-composed music and literature, we explore the myriad ways AI is being harnessed to both augment and autonomously create art. These developments represent a groundbreaking shift in artistic methodology, where AI's capacity to learn, interpret, and even mimic human creativity is leading to novel and often breathtaking artistic expressions.

However, this fusion of AI with human creativity also raises critical questions: Can AI truly be creative, or is it merely an echo of its human programmers? What does it mean for the future of art when machines can simulate and produce works that resonate with human audiences? This chapter seeks to navigate these questions, pondering the future of art in an AI-driven world.

AI's Role in Music, Visual Arts, and Literature

In Chapter 9 of "Echoes of Tomorrow: AI and the Future of Society," we explore the intricate and ever-evolving role of Artificial Intelligence (AI) in the realms of music, visual arts, and literature.

This deep dive reveals how AI is not just transforming these fields but also redefining the boundaries of creativity and artistic expression.

AI in Music

Composition and Production: AI algorithms are now capable of composing music, generating novel melodies, harmonies, and rhythms. These systems analyze vast databases of existing music to create new compositions that can mimic specific genres or even amalgamate styles in innovative ways.

Personalization and Recommendation: AI is used in music streaming services to analyze listening habits and recommend personalized playlists to users. This not only enhances user experience but also helps discover new artists and genres.

Sound Engineering: AI tools assist in sound mixing and mastering, tasks traditionally requiring human expertise. They can optimize sound quality by analyzing audio characteristics and making precise adjustments.

Live Performance: AI is starting to find its place in live performances, with algorithms capable of creating real-time music in response to changes in the environment or audience reactions.

AI in Visual Arts

Generative Art: AI systems, particularly those using Generative Adversarial Networks (GANs), are creating stunning visual artwork. These algorithms generate images by learning from vast datasets of paintings and photographs, often creating works that are indistinguishable from human-created art.

Enhancing Creativity: Artists are using AI as a collaborative tool to expand their creative possibilities. AI can suggest new visual elements, color schemes, and patterns, sparking new artistic ideas.

Restoration and Analysis: AI is used in analyzing and restoring artworks. By learning from historical data, AI can predict the original colors of faded paintings or suggest restoration techniques.

Interactive Art Installations: AI-driven installations offer immersive experiences, where art responds to and evolves with audience interactions, creating dynamic, ever-changing environments.

AI in Literature

Automated Writing: AI is being utilized to write poetry, stories, and even novels. These systems use natural language processing (NLP) to generate coherent and contextually relevant text, pushing the boundaries of automated storytelling.

Editorial Assistance: AI tools aid writers in grammar and style editing, refining their **work** with greater efficiency. Some AI systems provide suggestions on plot development and character consistency.

Literary Analysis: AI algorithms analyze literary works, offering insights into writing styles, thematic patterns, and cultural significance. This has applications in academic research and can aid in uncovering new perspectives on classic literature.

Personalized Reading Experiences: AI technology is being used to create interactive and personalized reading experiences, where the storyline can adapt based on reader choices, similar to a literary choose-your-own-adventure.

Ethical and Artistic Considerations

The integration of AI in art raises significant ethical and artistic considerations.

Authorship and Originality: Debates continue about whether AI-generated art can be considered original or if it merely reflects the datasets it was trained on. The question of authorship and copyright in AI-generated works is also a complex issue.

Cultural and Creative Impacts: There is concern that AI could homogenize art by replicating popular styles, potentially diminishing cultural diversity in artistic expression.

Economic Impacts: As AI becomes more prevalent in these fields, its impact on traditional roles and the economic aspects of the music, art, and literature industries must be considered.

AI's role in music, visual arts, and literature is both transformative and disruptive. It offers new tools for creative expression, challenging our traditional understanding of art and its creation. While AI opens up vast possibilities for innovation and exploration, it also brings forth critical questions about the nature of creativity, the role of the artist, and the future of artistic professions. Navigating this new landscape requires a balanced approach, acknowledging the potential of AI to enhance human creativity while being mindful of its implications on cultural expression and artistic value.

The Future of Creative Work in an AI World

In an AI-driven world, the landscape of creative work is undergoing a profound transformation. This detailed exploration focuses on how Artificial Intelligence (AI) is reshaping the nature of creative professions and what the future might hold for artists, writers, musicians, and other creative professionals.

AI as a Tool for Enhancing Creativity

Creative Collaboration with AI: Artists are increasingly using AI as a collaborative tool that enhances their creative process. AI algorithms can suggest new ideas, patterns, and possibilities that might not occur to a human mind, leading to novel artistic expressions.

Expanding the Horizons of Creativity: AI's ability to process and analyze vast amounts of data can inspire new forms of creative work, pushing the boundaries of traditional genres and mediums.

Personalization and Customization in Creative Work

Tailored Content Creation: In fields like music, literature, and art, AI can create personalized content based on individual preferences and histories. This leads to a more tailored and engaging consumer experience.

Customized User Experiences: AI's predictive capabilities enable the development of highly customized user experiences in digital media, video games, and interactive art.

Democratization of Creative Tools

Accessible Creative Platforms: AI-powered tools are democratizing creative expression, allowing individuals without formal training to create high-quality artistic works, write stories, or compose music.

Reducing Barriers to Entry: This democratization could lead to a more inclusive creative landscape, where diverse voices and stories are heard and appreciated.

The Changing Role of the Artist

Shifting from Creation to Curation: As AI takes on more of the traditional roles of generating content, the artist's role may shift towards curating and refining AI-generated material.

Ethical Considerations: Artists will increasingly grapple with ethical considerations, such as the authenticity and originality of AI-assisted work and the implications of using AI in their creative processes.

Implications for the Art Market

Redefining Value and Authenticity: The art market may need to reassess the notions of value and authenticity in the context of AI-generated art. Determining the worth and originality of artworks that are created with significant AI involvement presents new challenges.

New Market Dynamics: AI could also create new market dynamics, with AI-generated art becoming a genre of its own and potentially accessible to a broader audience.

AI in Film and Theater

Scriptwriting and Storytelling: AI's potential in scriptwriting and storytelling could see it becoming a valuable tool in film and theater, assisting writers in plot development and dialogue generation.

Special Effects and Animation: AI is already revolutionizing the field of special effects and animation, enabling more sophisticated and realistic creations with less manual effort.

Challenges and Concerns

Job Displacement Fears: There are concerns about job displacement as AI takes over certain creative tasks. This necessitates a reevaluation of skills and roles within creative industries.

Preserving Human Essence: In creative fields, maintaining the human essence in art is vital. Balancing AI's efficiency with the irreplaceable touch of human emotion and experience is a major challenge.

Education and Skill Development for a Creative AI Era

Adapting Educational Curricula: Educational institutions will need to adapt their curricula to equip students with the skills to work alongside AI, including AI literacy and data science skills.

Fostering Creativity and Critical Thinking: Emphasizing creativity, critical thinking, and emotional intelligence in education becomes crucial, as these are areas where AI cannot easily replicate human capabilities.

The Future of Publishing and Writing

AI-assisted Writing: In publishing and writing, AI tools can assist in editing, grammar checking, and even content generation, but the creative voice and vision of human authors remain central.

New Publishing Models: AI might give rise to new publishing models, including interactive and personalized storytelling.

The future of creative work in an AI world is one of collaboration between human ingenuity and machine intelligence. While AI brings tools and capabilities that can enhance and transform creative professions, it also presents challenges that need addressing, from ethical considerations to job displacement. Navigating this future will require a balanced approach that leverages AI's strengths while preserving the irreplaceable value of human creativity. The goal is not to replace human artists with machines but to empower them with new tools and possibilities, paving the way for an enriched, diverse, and dynamic creative landscape.

AI as a Collaborative Partner in Creative Processes

As we explore the role of Artificial Intelligence (AI) in the realm of creativity, a compelling narrative unfolds — AI as a collaborative partner in the creative process. This expansive view considers the ways AI is integrated into various forms of artistic expression, not as a replacement but as a complement to human creativity.

Enhancing Musical Composition and Production

In music, AI's role is evolving from a tool for basic composition to a sophisticated partner that understands and collaborates in the creative process.

Algorithmic Compositions: AI algorithms can analyze musical patterns and styles, offering composers new melodies, harmonies, and rhythms that can inspire or be integrated into their work.

Adaptive Music Production: AI can adapt music production techniques to the preferences of musicians and producers, facilitating more efficient and innovative production workflows.

The visual arts and design sectors are witnessing a profound transformation with AI's involvement.

Generative Art: AI algorithms, particularly Generative Adversarial Networks (GANs), create unique pieces of art by learning styles and elements from vast datasets of existing artwork. Artists use these outputs as a foundation or inspiration for their works.

Design Assistance: In design fields, AI assists in generating layouts, color schemes, and visual elements, speeding up the design process and allowing designers to focus on more nuanced aspects of their projects.

Literature and Writing

AI's integration into writing and literature is opening new avenues for storytelling and editing.

Story Development Tools: AI can suggest plot twists, character arcs, and even entire storylines, which writers can use as inspiration or incorporate into their work.

Editing and Language Processing: AI-powered tools aid in grammar, style, and consistency checks, streamlining the editing process without compromising the writer's original voice.

Film, Theatre, and Performance Arts

In film and theatre, AI's role is expanding beyond technical aspects to creative collaboration.

Script Analysis and Generation: AI tools analyze scripts for narrative structure and emotional impact, offering insights that can refine storytelling.

Virtual Actors and Digital Effects: AI-generated virtual actors and digital effects are used to create realistic scenes and characters, enhancing the visual storytelling experience.

AI in Digital and Interactive Media

AI is reshaping the landscape of digital and interactive media, including video games and virtual reality.

Dynamic Content Creation: In video games, AI generates dynamic content like landscapes and character dialogues, responding to player actions for a personalized experience.

Interactive Art Installations: AI-driven interactive installations react to audience inputs, creating immersive and evolving artistic experiences.

Collaborative Challenges and Opportunities

While AI presents numerous collaborative opportunities, it also brings challenges.

Creative Control and Originality: Determining the balance of creative control between AI and human artists raises questions about originality and authorship in AI-assisted works.

Ethical Considerations: The ethical implications of using AI in creative processes, such as potential biases in AI-generated content, require careful consideration.

The Future of AI in Creative Education

AI's role in creative education is becoming increasingly significant.

Teaching and Learning Tools: AI-powered tools in educational settings can provide personalized learning experiences, helping students develop their unique creative skills.

Bridging Technical and Creative Skills: Educators are incorporating AI into curricula to teach both technical skills related to AI and its applications in creative processes.

Collaboration Models between AI and Human Creatives

Various collaboration models are emerging between AI and human creatives.

Co-creation: In this model, AI and human artists work as co-creators, with AI providing inputs that are integrated into the final artwork.

Augmentation: Here, AI serves as an augmenting tool, enhancing the human artist's capabilities without directly influencing the creative output.

The integration of AI as a collaborative partner in creative processes heralds a new era in art and creativity. This partnership is not about machines overtaking human creativity but enhancing and expanding it. By leveraging AI's capabilities, artists, designers, writers, and creators can push the boundaries of traditional creativity, exploring new realms and narratives. However, navigating this partnership requires careful consideration of ethical, originality, and authorship issues. As we move forward, the collaboration between human creativity and AI promises to unlock unprecedented potential, leading to a richer, more diverse artistic landscape.

The Ethics and Aesthetics of AI-Generated Art

The emergence of AI-generated art represents a paradigm shift in the aesthetics and ethics of the art world. This extensive analysis delves into the complexities and nuances of this new art form, exploring the ethical considerations and aesthetic evaluations that AI-generated art provokes.

Defining AI-Generated Art

AI-generated art is created with the assistance of artificial intelligence algorithms, particularly those using machine learning techniques like neural networks. These systems are trained on large datasets of artworks and can produce images, sculptures, music, or even literary works.

Aesthetic Evaluation

Originality and Creativity: AI-generated art challenges our notions of originality. Traditionally, originality in art is closely tied to human creativity. With AI, the 'creativity' comes from algorithms processing and remixing existing data, raising questions about the originality of such works.

Human vs. Machine Art: There's an ongoing debate on whether AI-generated art can evoke the same depth of emotion and meaning as human-created art. This touches on the very essence of art – is it the expression of human experience, or can it be something autonomously created by a machine?

Ethical Considerations

Authorship and Copyright: Who owns an AI-created piece of art? Is it the developer of the AI, the user who inputted the prompts, or the AI itself? The legal framework around copyright in the context of AI art is still being shaped.

Transparency: There's an ethical need for transparency in AI art. Artists who use AI as a tool in their creative process should disclose the extent of AI involvement in their works.

Impact on the Art Community

Accessibility and Democratization: AI art tools can make art creation more accessible to those without formal training, potentially democratizing art creation and consumption. This can lead to a more inclusive art community.

Disruption of Traditional Art: The advent of AI-generated art could disrupt traditional art markets and economies, affecting artists, galleries, and collectors. It poses a challenge to existing value systems in the art world.

AI Art in the Marketplace

Monetization and Value: The sale of AI-generated art raises questions about its valuation. How do we appraise something that can be endlessly and effortlessly replicated by an algorithm?

New Avenues and Platforms: AI art is creating new platforms and markets, including digital art platforms and blockchain-based authentication methods.

The Role of AI in the Creative Process

AI as a Collaborative Tool: Many artists view AI as a tool that can enhance their creativity, offering new possibilities and perspectives in the creative process.

AI as an Autonomous Creator: When AI is set to create autonomously, it challenges the traditional role of the artist. This raises questions about the nature of creativity and whether it is an exclusively human trait.

Societal and Cultural Implications

Cultural Representation: AI-generated art, trained on datasets, may inadvertently perpetuate cultural biases or underrepresentation. Ensuring diverse and inclusive datasets is crucial.

Influence on Artistic Trends: AI's capability to analyze and generate art based on popular styles could influence and even dictate future artistic trends, impacting cultural diversity in art.

Future Directions and Challenges

Evolving AI Technologies: As AI technology evolves, so will its capabilities in art creation, continually pushing the boundaries of what is possible.

Regulatory and Ethical Frameworks: Developing comprehensive regulatory and ethical frameworks to guide the creation and use of AI art is an ongoing challenge.

The Intersection of Art and Technology

Interdisciplinary Collaboration: The field of AI art encourages collaboration between artists, technologists, ethicists, and legal experts, fostering an interdisciplinary approach.

Expanding Artistic Boundaries: AI challenges and expands the boundaries of traditional art, prompting us to reconsider our definitions and understandings of art.

AI-generated art is not just a technological marvel; it is a catalyst for profound discussions on the nature of creativity, the role of the artist, and the meaning of art itself. It raises ethical questions that straddle technology and art, prompting a reevaluation of how we perceive, value, and interact with art. As AI continues to advance, its role in art will undoubtedly grow, shaping new aesthetic landscapes and ethical paradigms. In this context, embracing AI-generated art requires a careful balancing act, celebrating innovation while critically examining its implications for art and society.

Chapter 10
AI and Space Exploration

Chapter 10 of "Echoes of Tomorrow: AI and the Future of Society" delves into the captivating realm where Artificial Intelligence (AI) intersects with space exploration, a frontier of human endeavor that has always been synonymous with innovation, discovery, and the relentless pursuit of knowledge. In this chapter, we embark on a journey to explore how AI technologies are revolutionizing the way we understand, navigate, and explore the cosmos.

From autonomous rovers on distant planets to predictive analytics for spacecraft trajectories, AI is playing an increasingly integral role in every aspect of space exploration. As humanity sets its sights on ambitious missions to the Moon, Mars, and beyond, AI serves as a critical enabler, augmenting human capabilities and expanding the scope of what is achievable.

In this introductory exploration, we'll delve into the ways AI is reshaping space exploration, from enhancing the efficiency and safety of missions to unlocking new frontiers of scientific discovery. We'll also confront the ethical and philosophical implications of relying on AI in the vast expanse of space, pondering questions of autonomy, responsibility, and the human quest for understanding the universe. Join us as we venture into the cosmos, guided by the transformative power of AI, in our relentless pursuit of the unknown.

AI in Navigating the Cosmos

Artificial Intelligence (AI) has emerged as an indispensable tool in the endeavor to explore and navigate the vast expanse of the cosmos. In this detailed exploration, we uncover the myriad ways AI is revolutionizing space exploration, from guiding spacecraft through the depths of space to aiding in the discovery of new celestial bodies.

Autonomous Spacecraft Navigation

One of the most significant applications of AI in space exploration is in the navigation of spacecraft. Traditional spacecraft navigation relies on pre-programmed instructions and human intervention. However, with the introduction of AI, spacecraft can now autonomously navigate through space, making decisions in real-time based on sensor data and mission objectives.

Autonomous Rovers: On planetary surfaces such as Mars, AI-powered rovers like NASA's Curiosity and Perseverance can navigate complex terrain, avoid obstacles, and even make decisions about which areas to explore based on scientific criteria.

Deep Space Probes: Deep space probes like Voyager and New Horizons utilize AI algorithms to adjust their trajectories, perform course corrections, and navigate through asteroid belts and other hazards encountered during their missions.

Predictive Analytics for Spacecraft Trajectories

AI is also instrumental in predicting and optimizing spacecraft trajectories, ensuring missions are executed with precision and efficiency.

Trajectory Planning: AI algorithms analyze vast amounts of data, including gravitational forces, planetary orbits, and atmospheric conditions, to calculate optimal trajectories for spacecraft. This allows missions to be planned with greater accuracy and efficiency.

Collision Avoidance: AI-powered systems monitor spacecraft trajectories in real-time, predicting potential collisions with space debris or other celestial objects and recommending course adjustments to avoid collisions.

Autonomous Space Telescopes and Observatories

AI is revolutionizing the way space telescopes and observatories operate, enabling them to autonomously select and prioritize observations based on scientific goals and data analysis.

Automated Target Selection: AI algorithms analyze data from space telescopes like the Hubble Space Telescope and the James Webb Space Telescope to identify interesting celestial objects and phenomena. They can then autonomously select targets for further observation based on predefined criteria.

Real-Time Data Analysis: AI systems onboard space telescopes analyze data as it is collected, identifying patterns, anomalies, and interesting phenomena in real-time. This allows for rapid scientific discoveries and enables telescopes to respond dynamically to changing conditions in the cosmos.

AI in Extraterrestrial Exploration

As humanity explores the possibility of extraterrestrial life and habitats, AI is playing a crucial role in analyzing data and identifying potential signs of life on other planets and moons.

Bioinformatics and Exobiology: AI algorithms analyze data collected by spacecraft and rovers to search for evidence of microbial life or habitable conditions on other planets and moons. This includes analyzing soil samples, atmospheric compositions, and geological features for signs of biological activity.

AI-Powered Instruments: Future missions to Europa, Enceladus, and other potentially habitable worlds may be equipped with AI-powered instruments designed to detect signs of life in subsurface oceans or beneath the icy crusts of these moons.

Ethical Considerations and Challenges

While AI holds tremendous promise for the future of space exploration, it also raises important ethical considerations and challenges that must be addressed.

Autonomy and Responsibility: As spacecraft become increasingly autonomous, questions arise about who is ultimately responsible for their actions and decisions. Establishing clear guidelines and protocols for AI-controlled spacecraft is essential to ensure mission safety and success.

Data Privacy and Security: AI systems onboard spacecraft collect vast amounts of data, including sensitive scientific data and potentially personally identifiable information. Ensuring the privacy and security of this data is paramount to maintaining public trust in space exploration missions.

AI Bias and Fairness: AI algorithms are only as good as the data they are trained on. Ensuring AI systems are free from bias and capable of making fair and objective decisions is critical to the success of space exploration missions and the integrity of scientific research.

AI is transforming the way we explore and navigate the cosmos, enabling spacecraft to operate autonomously, optimizing mission trajectories, and uncovering new insights into the universe. As AI technology continues to advance, its role in space exploration will only become more prominent, unlocking new frontiers of scientific discovery and expanding humanity's understanding of the cosmos. However, as we venture further into space with AI as our guide, it is essential to address the ethical considerations and challenges associated with its use to ensure the responsible and equitable exploration of the universe.

The Role of AI in Future Space Missions

Artificial Intelligence (AI) stands poised to revolutionize future space missions, playing a pivotal role in enhancing efficiency, autonomy, and scientific discovery. In this comprehensive exploration, we delve into the multifaceted ways AI is poised to shape the future of space exploration.

Autonomous Exploration and Navigation

AI will enable spacecraft to operate autonomously, making real-time decisions based on sensor data and mission objectives. This autonomy is crucial for missions to distant celestial bodies where communication delays prevent direct human intervention.

Autonomous Rovers: Future Mars rovers equipped with AI algorithms will navigate complex terrain, analyze rock formations, and determine optimal paths for exploration without constant input from Earth.

Deep Space Probes: AI will enable deep space probes to adjust their trajectories, perform course corrections, and avoid hazards encountered during long-duration missions to distant planets, asteroids, and comets.

Advanced Data Analysis and Interpretation

AI will revolutionize the way we analyze and interpret data collected during space missions, accelerating scientific discoveries and unlocking new insights into the cosmos.

Real-Time Data Processing: AI algorithms onboard spacecraft will analyze data as it is collected, identifying patterns, anomalies, and scientifically significant phenomena in real-time. This enables rapid decision-making and facilitates timely responses to dynamic conditions in space.

Predictive Analytics: AI will predict and model complex phenomena such as solar flares, cosmic ray events, and planetary atmospheres, providing valuable insights for mission planning and risk mitigation.

Adaptive Systems and Instruments

AI-powered adaptive systems and instruments will enable spacecraft to dynamically respond to changing conditions and optimize their performance in real-time.

Adaptive Optics: Space telescopes equipped with AI-powered adaptive optics will compensate for atmospheric distortions, enhancing image resolution and clarity for astronomical observations.

Self-Healing Systems: AI will enable spacecraft to diagnose and repair hardware failures autonomously, prolonging mission lifetimes and reducing the risk of mission failure due to technical malfunctions.

Autonomous Science Operations

AI will enable spacecraft to conduct autonomous scientific investigations, prioritizing observations, and experiments based on scientific objectives and data analysis.

Automated Target Selection: AI algorithms will analyze data collected by telescopes and sensors, identifying scientifically interesting targets for further investigation. This accelerates the pace of scientific discovery by streamlining the process of target selection and observation planning.

Intelligent Sampling and Analysis: Future missions to celestial bodies such as asteroids and moons will utilize AI to autonomously select and analyze samples, optimizing resource utilization and scientific return.

Enhanced Mission Planning and Decision Support

AI-powered systems will assist mission planners and operators in optimizing mission trajectories, scheduling operations, and mitigating risks.

Mission Planning and Optimization: AI algorithms will generate optimized mission trajectories, taking into account mission objectives, spacecraft capabilities, and celestial mechanics. This ensures efficient resource utilization and maximizes scientific return.

Risk Assessment and Mitigation: AI will assess and mitigate mission risks by analyzing data from spacecraft sensors, predicting potential hazards, and recommending proactive measures to safeguard mission success.

Ethical Considerations and Challenges

As AI assumes a greater role in future space missions, ethical considerations and challenges must be addressed to ensure responsible and equitable exploration of the cosmos.

Autonomy and Accountability: Clarifying the roles and responsibilities of AI-controlled spacecraft is essential to ensure accountability and mitigate the risk of unintended consequences.

Data Privacy and Security: Protecting sensitive scientific data collected during space missions from unauthorized access or misuse is paramount to maintaining the integrity of scientific research and safeguarding privacy.

AI Bias and Fairness: Ensuring AI algorithms are free from bias and capable of making fair and objective decisions is critical to the success and credibility of space exploration missions.

The integration of AI into future space missions holds tremendous promise for advancing scientific discovery, expanding our understanding of the cosmos, and paving the way for humanity's continued exploration of space. By leveraging AI's capabilities in autonomous navigation, advanced data analysis, adaptive systems, and decision support, future space missions will be more efficient, productive, and scientifically rewarding. However, addressing the ethical considerations and challenges associated with AI in space exploration is essential to ensure the responsible and equitable exploration of the universe. As we venture further into space with AI as our guide, it is imperative to uphold principles of transparency, accountability, and fairness to ensure the success and integrity of future space missions.

AI in Astrobiology and Extraterrestrial Research

The search for extraterrestrial life and the study of astrobiology represent some of the most profound and captivating quests in the field of space exploration. Artificial Intelligence (AI) is poised to revolutionize these endeavors, offering advanced capabilities in data analysis, pattern recognition, and decision-making. In this comprehensive exploration, we delve into the role of AI in astrobiology and extraterrestrial research, uncovering how AI is reshaping our understanding of life beyond Earth.

Automated Data Analysis

AI algorithms are invaluable in the analysis of vast datasets collected during astrobiological research missions. These algorithms can sift through terabytes of data, identify patterns, and detect anomalies that may signify the presence of extraterrestrial life.

Planetary Data Analysis: AI systems analyze data from spacecraft missions, such as spectral data from planetary surfaces or atmospheric compositions, to identify potential biosignatures indicative of life.

Exoplanet Characterization: AI algorithms analyze light curves and spectroscopic data from telescopes to characterize exoplanets and assess their potential habitability.

Autonomous Exploration

AI enables autonomous exploration of celestial bodies, allowing spacecraft to make real-time decisions based on onboard data and mission objectives. This autonomy is crucial for missions to distant planets and moons where communication delays make direct human intervention impractical.

Robotic Exploration: AI-powered rovers and landers can navigate challenging terrain, collect samples, and conduct experiments autonomously, reducing the need for constant human oversight.

Autonomous Probes: Deep space probes equipped with AI can adjust their trajectories, perform course corrections, and adapt to unexpected conditions encountered during long-duration missions.

Remote Sensing and Instrumentation

AI enhances the capabilities of remote sensing instruments used in astrobiology and extraterrestrial research, enabling more precise measurements and analysis of planetary surfaces and atmospheres.

Machine Learning in Spectroscopy: AI algorithms analyze spectral data to identify organic compounds, minerals, and other substances indicative of past or present life.

Image Analysis: AI-powered image analysis tools can detect subtle features on planetary surfaces, such as impact craters, riverbeds, or sedimentary layers, that may provide clues about past environmental conditions.

Predictive Modeling and Simulation

AI facilitates predictive modeling and simulation of planetary environments, enabling scientists to simulate conditions on other worlds and assess their potential habitability.

Climate Modeling: AI algorithms simulate climate patterns and atmospheric dynamics on exoplanets and planetary bodies, providing insights into their potential habitability and evolutionary history.

Geological Modeling: AI-powered geological models reconstruct past environments on planetary surfaces, helping scientists understand the history of water, volcanism, and tectonics on other worlds.

Bioinformatics and Life Detection

AI is instrumental in bioinformatics and life detection studies, helping scientists analyze genetic data, identify biomarkers, and search for signs of life in extreme environments on Earth and beyond.

DNA Sequencing Analysis: AI algorithms analyze DNA sequences to identify genes associated with extremophiles and other organisms that thrive in harsh environments, providing insights into the potential for life on other planets.

Biosignature Detection: AI systems search for biosignatures, such as methane plumes or unusual atmospheric compositions, that may indicate the presence of life on other worlds.

Challenges and Ethical Considerations

While AI holds tremendous promise for astrobiology and extraterrestrial research, it also presents challenges and ethical considerations that must be addressed.

Data Quality and Interpretation: Ensuring the accuracy and reliability of data used in AI algorithms is essential to prevent false positives and ensure robust scientific conclusions.

Planetary Protection: AI-driven spacecraft must adhere to strict planetary protection protocols to prevent contamination of other worlds with Earthly microbes and protect the integrity of potential biospheres.

Ethical Use of AI: Ethical considerations surrounding the use of AI in astrobiology include issues of transparency, accountability, and bias in algorithmic decision-making.

The integration of AI into astrobiology and extraterrestrial research represents a paradigm shift in our approach to understanding the potential for life beyond Earth. By harnessing the power of AI for automated data analysis, autonomous exploration, predictive modeling, and life detection, scientists are unlocking new insights into the mysteries of the cosmos. However, addressing the challenges and ethical considerations associated with AI in astrobiology is essential to ensure the responsible and ethical pursuit of knowledge about life beyond our planet. As we continue to explore the cosmos with AI as our guide, we embark on a journey of discovery that may one day reveal the existence of life beyond Earth and our place in the universe.

AI-Powered Robotics in Space Exploration

The marriage of Artificial Intelligence (AI) and robotics has revolutionized space exploration, enabling autonomous and intelligent systems to navigate, explore, and conduct experiments in the harsh environments of space. In this comprehensive analysis, we delve into the multifaceted role of AI-powered robotics in advancing our understanding of the cosmos and pushing the boundaries of space exploration.

Autonomous Spacecraft and Rovers

AI-powered robotics play a crucial role in the design and operation of autonomous spacecraft and rovers, enabling them to navigate and explore celestial bodies with minimal human intervention.

Autonomous Navigation: Spacecraft equipped with AI algorithms can navigate complex terrain, avoid obstacles, and adapt to unforeseen obstacles or hazards encountered during missions.

Exploration Efficiency: AI-powered rovers like NASA's Curiosity and Perseverance can conduct scientific experiments, collect samples, and analyze data autonomously, maximizing the scientific return of space missions.

Adaptive Systems and Decision-Making

AI enables robots to make real-time decisions based on sensory input and mission objectives, allowing them to adapt to changing conditions and unforeseen challenges encountered during space missions.

Adaptive Control Systems: AI algorithms enable robots to dynamically adjust their behavior and responses based on sensor data, ensuring optimal performance in dynamic and uncertain environments.

Machine Learning Models: Robots equipped with machine learning models can learn from experience and improve their decision-making capabilities over time, enhancing their efficiency and adaptability in space missions.

Onboard Science and Experimentation

AI-powered robots serve as valuable scientific instruments in space exploration, conducting experiments, analyzing data, and collecting samples to further our understanding of the cosmos.

Laboratory Capabilities: AI-powered robots equipped with scientific instruments can perform experiments and analyses in situ, providing real-time insights into planetary geology, chemistry, and atmospheric conditions.

Sample Collection and Analysis: Robots can collect samples from planetary surfaces or subsurface environments and analyze them onboard, identifying potential biosignatures or valuable resources for future exploration.

Remote Sensing and Instrumentation

AI enhances the capabilities of remote sensing instruments used in space exploration, enabling robots to gather detailed information about distant celestial bodies and phenomena.

Image Processing: AI algorithms analyze images collected by robotic cameras and sensors, identifying interesting features, anomalies, or scientifically significant phenomena on planetary surfaces.

Spectroscopic Analysis: Robots equipped with spectroscopic instruments can analyze the composition of planetary atmospheres, surface materials, and geological formations, providing insights into their origin and evolution.

Collaborative and Swarm Robotics

AI enables collaborative and swarm robotics approaches in space exploration, allowing multiple robots to work together to accomplish complex tasks and objectives.

Collaborative Exploration: Teams of robots can collaborate to explore large areas or complex environments more efficiently, sharing information and coordinating their actions to achieve common goals.

Distributed Sensing and Mapping: Swarm robotics enables distributed sensing and mapping of planetary surfaces or subsurface environments, providing high-resolution data and insights into geological features and resources.

Challenges and Future Directions

While AI-powered robotics hold immense promise for space exploration, they also present challenges and opportunities for further advancement.

Robustness and Reliability: Ensuring the robustness and reliability of AI algorithms and robotic systems in the harsh conditions of space is crucial to the success of future missions.

Interplanetary Communication: Developing efficient communication protocols and data transmission methods for AI-powered robots operating in remote or hostile environments is essential for mission success.

Ethical Considerations: Addressing ethical considerations surrounding the use of AI in space exploration, including issues of autonomy, accountability, and transparency, is essential to ensure responsible and ethical conduct of space missions.

AI-powered robotics represent a transformative force in space exploration, enabling autonomous and intelligent systems to navigate, explore, and conduct experiments in the cosmos. By harnessing the capabilities of AI for autonomous navigation, adaptive decision-making, onboard science, and collaborative exploration, robots are pushing the boundaries of what is possible in space exploration. As we continue to develop and deploy AI-powered robots in future space missions, we embark on a journey of discovery that promises to unlock new insights into the mysteries of the universe and pave the way for humanity's continued exploration and colonization of space.

Chapter 11
AI and the Future of Governance

Chapter 11 of "Echoes of Tomorrow: AI and the Future of Society" explores the transformative potential of Artificial Intelligence (AI) in shaping the future of governance. In this introduction, we embark on a journey to uncover the profound implications of AI for governance systems worldwide.

AI holds the promise of revolutionizing the way governments operate, make decisions, and interact with their citizens. From enhancing administrative efficiency to improving public service delivery and policymaking, AI has the potential to transform every aspect of governance.

In this chapter, we will examine the diverse applications of AI in governance, ranging from predictive analytics for policy formulation to chatbots for citizen engagement and decision support systems for public administration. We will also explore the ethical, social, and political implications of AI-driven governance, addressing concerns such as transparency, accountability, and algorithmic bias.

As governments around the world grapple with the challenges of the 21st century, AI offers unprecedented opportunities to address complex problems and build more inclusive, responsive, and efficient governance systems. Join us as we delve into the future of governance in the age of AI, exploring the possibilities and pitfalls of this transformative technology.

AI in Public Administration and Services

Artificial Intelligence (AI) is poised to revolutionize public administration and services, offering transformative capabilities that enhance efficiency, effectiveness, and citizen satisfaction. In this comprehensive exploration, we delve into the multifaceted role of AI in reshaping the delivery of public services and the functioning of government institutions.

Administrative Efficiency and Automation

AI streamlines administrative processes and tasks, reducing manual effort and enabling public servants to focus on higher-value activities.

Document Processing: AI-powered systems automate document processing tasks such as data entry, classification, and extraction, reducing administrative burden and processing times for government agencies.

Workflow Optimization: AI algorithms analyze workflow patterns and optimize resource allocation, ensuring tasks are prioritized and completed efficiently within government departments.

Predictive Analytics for Policy Formulation

AI enables governments to harness vast amounts of data to inform evidence-based policy decisions and anticipate future trends and challenges.

Policy Modeling: AI-powered predictive analytics models forecast the potential impact of policy interventions, enabling policymakers to make informed decisions and allocate resources effectively.

Risk Assessment: AI algorithms analyze data from various sources, including demographics, socioeconomic indicators, and historical trends, to identify emerging risks and vulnerabilities in society.

Citizen Engagement and Service Delivery

AI enhances citizen engagement and improves the delivery of public services by providing personalized, responsive, and accessible solutions.

Chatbots and Virtual Assistants: AI-powered chatbots and virtual assistants interact with citizens, providing information, answering queries, and guiding them through government services and procedures.

Personalized Recommendations: AI algorithms analyze citizen data and preferences to offer personalized recommendations for services, benefits, and opportunities tailored to individual needs.

Decision Support Systems

AI-driven decision support systems empower government leaders and policymakers with data-driven insights and recommendations to guide strategic planning and decision-making.

Data Analysis and Visualization: AI algorithms process and analyze large datasets, generating visualizations and insights that help policymakers understand complex issues and trends.

Scenario Planning: AI-powered simulations and scenario planning tools enable policymakers to explore different policy options and their potential outcomes, facilitating informed decision-making and risk management.

Transparency and Accountability

While AI offers significant benefits for public administration, it also raises important considerations regarding transparency, accountability, and ethical governance.

Algorithmic Transparency: Ensuring transparency in AI algorithms and decision-making processes is essential to build trust and accountability in government systems.

Ethical Use of Data: Governments must uphold ethical principles and safeguard citizen privacy and rights when collecting, storing, and using data for AI applications in public administration.

Challenges and Considerations

Despite its potential, AI in public administration also presents challenges and considerations that must be addressed for responsible and effective implementation.

Skills and Capacity Building: Building AI capabilities and digital literacy among public servants is crucial to harness the full potential of AI in government operations.

Equity and Accessibility: Governments must ensure that AI-driven services and solutions are accessible to all citizens, regardless of socioeconomic status or technological literacy.

Regulatory Frameworks: Establishing clear regulatory frameworks and guidelines for AI applications in public administration is essential to mitigate risks and ensure ethical and responsible use of AI technologies.

AI is poised to transform public administration and services, offering unprecedented opportunities to improve efficiency, effectiveness, and citizen satisfaction in government operations. By harnessing the power of AI for administrative automation, predictive analytics, citizen engagement, and decision support, governments can build more responsive, transparent, and accountable governance systems. However, addressing challenges related to transparency, accountability, and ethical governance is essential to ensure the responsible and equitable deployment of AI in public administration. As governments embrace AI-driven solutions to address complex challenges, they must uphold principles of fairness, equity, and inclusivity to build trust and confidence in government institutions and services.

The Impact of AI on Global Politics and Diplomacy

Artificial Intelligence (AI) is fundamentally transforming global politics and diplomacy, reshaping the dynamics of international relations, decision-making processes, and geopolitical strategies. In this comprehensive analysis, we delve into the multifaceted ways in which AI is influencing and shaping the landscape of global politics and diplomacy.

AI in Geopolitical Analysis and Decision-Making

AI-powered analytical tools are revolutionizing geopolitical analysis, providing policymakers and diplomats with valuable insights and predictive capabilities to navigate complex international issues.

Data Mining and Analysis: AI algorithms process vast amounts of data from diverse sources, including social media, news articles, and satellite imagery, to identify patterns, trends, and emerging geopolitical risks.

Predictive Modeling: AI-powered predictive analytics models forecast geopolitical events, such as elections, conflicts, and economic trends, enabling governments to anticipate challenges and formulate proactive strategies.

AI in Diplomatic Communication and Negotiation

AI technologies are enhancing diplomatic communication and negotiation processes, facilitating dialogue, mediation, and conflict resolution between nations.

Language Translation: AI-powered translation tools enable diplomats to communicate effectively across language barriers, facilitating dialogue and negotiation in multilateral settings.

Sentiment Analysis: AI algorithms analyze diplomatic communications and media sentiment to gauge public opinion and sentiment on international issues, informing diplomatic strategies and messaging.

AI in Cybersecurity and Information Warfare

AI is playing an increasingly significant role in cybersecurity and information warfare, shaping the dynamics of conflict and competition in the digital domain.

Cyber Defense: AI-powered cybersecurity systems detect and respond to cyber threats in real-time, protecting critical infrastructure and national security interests from cyber attacks and espionage.

Disinformation Detection: AI algorithms analyze online content to identify and counter disinformation campaigns, protecting democratic institutions and public discourse from manipulation and interference.

AI in Military Strategy and Warfare

AI technologies are transforming military strategy and warfare, enabling nations to develop autonomous weapons systems, conduct predictive analysis of military operations, and enhance battlefield decision-making.

Autonomous Weapons: AI-powered drones, missiles, and autonomous vehicles are reshaping the nature of warfare, raising ethical and legal questions about the use of lethal autonomous weapons systems (LAWS) and their implications for international security.

Predictive Analysis: AI algorithms analyze military data to predict enemy movements, assess battlefield conditions, and optimize military operations, providing commanders with valuable insights for strategic decision-making.

AI in Global Governance and International Institutions

AI is influencing the functioning of global governance structures and international institutions, facilitating collaboration, coordination, and decision-making on transnational issues.

Multilateral Cooperation: AI-powered platforms and tools enable international organizations and governments to collaborate on global challenges, such as climate change, pandemic response, and humanitarian crises, fostering multilateralism and cooperation.

Regulatory Frameworks: International efforts are underway to develop regulatory frameworks and norms for the responsible use of AI in global governance, addressing issues such as data privacy, algorithmic bias, and human rights in AI-driven decision-making processes.

Ethical and Legal Implications

The widespread adoption of AI in global politics and diplomacy raises important ethical and legal considerations that must be addressed to ensure responsible and equitable use of AI technologies.

Ethical Decision-Making: AI systems must be programmed to adhere to ethical principles and norms, respecting human rights, dignity, and autonomy in diplomatic and political decision-making processes.

International Law: The development and deployment of AI technologies in military and diplomatic contexts must comply with international humanitarian law, human rights law, and arms control agreements to prevent unintended consequences and mitigate risks of conflict escalation.

Artificial Intelligence is profoundly impacting global politics and diplomacy, transforming the dynamics of international relations, decision-making processes, and geopolitical strategies. By harnessing the power of AI for geopolitical analysis, diplomatic communication, cybersecurity, military strategy, and global governance, nations can navigate complex international issues and challenges more effectively. However, addressing ethical, legal, and strategic implications of AI in global politics and diplomacy is essential to ensure responsible and equitable use of AI technologies and promote stability, cooperation, and peace in the international community. As nations adapt to the realities of AI-driven geopolitics, they must uphold principles of transparency, accountability, and respect for human rights to build trust and confidence in diplomatic and political institutions and promote a more secure and prosperous world for all.

AI in Law Enforcement and Judicial Systems

Artificial Intelligence (AI) is increasingly being integrated into law enforcement and judicial systems worldwide, offering a range of capabilities that enhance crime prevention, investigation, and adjudication processes. In this comprehensive analysis, we explore the multifaceted ways in which AI is transforming the landscape of law enforcement and judicial systems, addressing both the opportunities and challenges associated with its implementation.

Crime Prediction and Prevention

AI technologies play a crucial role in crime prediction and prevention, leveraging data analytics and machine learning algorithms to identify patterns, trends, and potential threats.

Predictive Policing: AI-powered predictive analytics models analyze historical crime data, demographic information, and other relevant factors to forecast where and when crimes are likely to occur, enabling law enforcement agencies to allocate resources effectively and deploy preventive measures proactively.

Risk Assessment: AI algorithms assess the likelihood of individuals reoffending or engaging in criminal behavior, helping judges and probation officers make informed decisions about pretrial release, sentencing, and parole supervision.

Enhanced Investigation and Evidence Analysis

AI-powered tools enhance the efficiency and effectiveness of criminal investigations, enabling law enforcement agencies to process and analyze large volumes of data and evidence more quickly and accurately.

Digital Forensics: AI algorithms analyze digital evidence, such as emails, social media posts, and encrypted communications, to identify relevant information and connections in criminal investigations, helping investigators gather evidence and build cases more efficiently.

Facial Recognition: AI-powered facial recognition systems assist law enforcement agencies in identifying suspects and persons of interest from surveillance footage and public databases, facilitating the apprehension of criminals and the rescue of missing persons.

Improved Public Safety and Emergency Response

AI technologies contribute to improving public safety and emergency response efforts by providing real-time insights and decision support to law enforcement and emergency services personnel.

Intelligent Video Analytics: AI-powered video analytics systems monitor surveillance footage and detect suspicious activities or events in real-time, enabling law enforcement agencies to respond promptly to emergencies and threats to public safety.

Natural Language Processing: AI-driven chatbots and virtual assistants provide citizens with access to emergency services, information, and assistance during crises and natural disasters, enhancing communication and coordination in emergency response efforts.

Legal Research and Case Management

AI-powered tools assist legal professionals in conducting legal research, analyzing case law, and managing caseloads more efficiently, improving the effectiveness and fairness of the judicial process.

Legal Research Assistants: AI-powered legal research platforms analyze vast databases of case law, statutes, and legal documents to identify relevant precedents, statutes, and legal arguments, assisting lawyers and judges in preparing cases and making legal decisions.

Case Management Systems: AI-driven case management systems automate routine administrative tasks, such as scheduling, document management, and case tracking, enabling legal professionals to focus more time and attention on substantive legal work and client representation.

Ethical and Legal Considerations

While AI offers significant benefits for law enforcement and judicial systems, its implementation raises important ethical, legal, and social considerations that must be addressed to ensure responsible and equitable use of AI technologies.

Algorithmic Bias and Fairness: AI algorithms may exhibit bias or discrimination against certain individuals or groups, leading to unfair or disproportionate outcomes in law enforcement and judicial decision-making processes. Addressing algorithmic bias requires transparency, accountability, and ongoing monitoring and evaluation of AI systems to ensure fairness and equity.

Privacy and Data Protection: AI technologies often rely on large volumes of personal data, raising concerns about privacy, data protection, and surveillance. Governments and law enforcement agencies must establish robust legal frameworks and safeguards to protect individuals' privacy rights and ensure responsible use of personal data in AI-driven law enforcement activities.

Challenges and Future Directions

Despite the potential benefits of AI in law enforcement and judicial systems, several challenges and considerations must be addressed to realize its full potential and mitigate potential risks.

Training and Education: Law enforcement officers, legal professionals, and judicial officials require training and education to understand AI technologies, their capabilities, and limitations, and to effectively integrate them into their workflow and decision-making processes.

Regulatory Frameworks: Governments and regulatory bodies must develop clear and comprehensive regulatory frameworks and guidelines for the responsible use of AI in law enforcement and judicial systems, ensuring compliance with legal and ethical standards and protecting individuals' rights and liberties.

Artificial Intelligence is transforming law enforcement and judicial systems, offering a range of capabilities that enhance crime prevention, investigation, and adjudication processes. By leveraging AI technologies for crime prediction, evidence analysis, emergency response, legal research, and case management, law enforcement agencies and judicial systems can improve public safety, enhance efficiency, and ensure fairness and justice in the administration of the law. However, addressing ethical, legal, and social considerations associated with the implementation of AI in law enforcement and judicial systems is essential to ensure responsible and equitable use of AI technologies and uphold fundamental principles of fairness, transparency, and human rights. As governments and legal institutions continue to navigate the complexities of AI-driven law enforcement and judicial practices, they must prioritize ethical and responsible AI governance to build trust and confidence in the justice system and protect the rights and liberties of all individuals.

AI and the Future of Democratic Processes

Artificial Intelligence (AI) is poised to fundamentally reshape democratic processes worldwide, offering opportunities to enhance citizen engagement, improve governance, and strengthen democratic institutions. In this comprehensive analysis, we explore the multifaceted ways in which AI is transforming the landscape of democratic processes, addressing both the promises and challenges associated with its integration into democratic systems.

Enhancing Citizen Engagement

AI technologies have the potential to revolutionize citizen engagement in democratic processes, fostering greater participation, transparency, and accountability.

Online Platforms and Social Media: AI-powered platforms analyze user data and preferences to personalize content and recommendations, facilitating informed political discourse and engagement among citizens.

Chatbots and Virtual Assistants: AI-driven chatbots and virtual assistants provide citizens with access to information, services, and representatives, enhancing communication and interaction between government institutions and the public.

Improving Electoral Processes

AI offers innovative solutions to improve the integrity, efficiency, and accessibility of electoral processes, ensuring fair and transparent elections.

Voter Registration and Verification: AI algorithms verify voter eligibility and detect fraudulent activities, enhancing the accuracy and security of voter registration processes.

Election Monitoring and Security: AI-powered systems monitor electoral activities, detect irregularities or anomalies, and enhance cybersecurity measures to protect electoral infrastructure from cyber threats and interference.

Augmenting Policy Formulation and Decision-Making

AI technologies provide valuable insights and decision support tools to policymakers, enabling evidence-based policy formulation and strategic decision-making.

Predictive Analytics: AI-powered predictive analytics models forecast the potential impact of policy interventions, enabling policymakers to anticipate challenges, identify opportunities, and allocate resources effectively.

Data-driven Governance: AI algorithms analyze vast datasets, including demographic information, socioeconomic indicators, and public opinion polls, to inform policy decisions and prioritize government initiatives based on citizen needs and preferences.

Strengthening Government Transparency and Accountability

AI enhances government transparency and accountability by providing mechanisms for monitoring, oversight, and public scrutiny of government activities and decision-making processes.

Open Data Initiatives: AI technologies analyze government data and make it accessible to the public through open data platforms, empowering citizens, journalists, and civil society organizations to hold government institutions accountable for their actions and expenditures.

Algorithmic Governance: AI-driven algorithms transparently process and analyze government data to inform decision-making processes, enabling citizens to understand the rationale behind government policies and actions.

Addressing Disinformation and Misinformation

AI technologies play a critical role in combating disinformation and misinformation, safeguarding the integrity of democratic processes and public discourse.

Content Moderation: AI-powered content moderation systems detect and remove false or harmful content from online platforms, mitigating the spread of misinformation and protecting the integrity of public discourse.

Fact-Checking and Verification: AI algorithms analyze news articles and social media posts to verify the accuracy and credibility of information, helping citizens distinguish between factual content and misinformation.

Challenges and Ethical Considerations

While AI offers significant potential to enhance democratic processes, its integration into democratic systems also raises important challenges and ethical considerations that must be addressed to ensure responsible and equitable use of AI technologies.

Privacy and Data Protection: AI technologies often rely on large volumes of personal data, raising concerns about privacy, data protection, and surveillance. Governments must establish robust legal frameworks and safeguards to protect individuals' privacy rights and ensure responsible use of personal data in AI-driven democratic processes.

Algorithmic Bias and Fairness: AI algorithms may exhibit bias or discrimination against certain individuals or groups, leading to unfair or discriminatory outcomes in democratic decision-making processes. Addressing algorithmic bias requires transparency, accountability, and ongoing monitoring and evaluation of AI systems to ensure fairness and equity.

Artificial Intelligence is reshaping the future of democratic processes, offering opportunities to enhance citizen engagement, improve governance, and strengthen democratic institutions. By leveraging AI technologies for citizen engagement, electoral processes, policy formulation, transparency, and combating disinformation, democratic societies can foster greater participation, accountability, and trust in government institutions. However, addressing challenges related to privacy, algorithmic bias, and ethical governance is essential to ensure responsible and equitable use of AI technologies in democratic systems. As governments and civil society organizations navigate the complexities of AI-driven democracy, they must prioritize ethical and responsible AI governance to protect democratic values, safeguard fundamental rights, and promote inclusive and participatory governance for all citizens.

Chapter 12
AI in Personal Development and Self-Improvement

In this chapter, we delve into the diverse ways in which AI is transforming personal development, including:

Personalized Learning: AI-powered platforms analyze individual learning styles and preferences to tailor educational content and experiences, fostering lifelong learning and skill development.

Health and Wellness: AI-driven health and wellness apps monitor physical activity, sleep patterns, and emotional well-being, providing personalized insights and recommendations to promote holistic health and self-care.

Productivity and Time Management: AI tools assist individuals in optimizing their productivity and managing their time more effectively, helping them achieve their goals and fulfill their potential.

Emotional Intelligence: AI applications facilitate emotional intelligence development through virtual coaching, mindfulness exercises, and mood tracking, empowering individuals to cultivate resilience, empathy, and self-awareness.

Goal Setting and Habit Formation: AI-driven goal-setting platforms and habit-tracking apps support individuals in setting meaningful goals, tracking progress, and cultivating positive habits for personal and professional growth.

As we navigate the possibilities and challenges of AI in personal development and self-improvement, we embark on a journey to discover how AI technologies can empower individuals to unlock their full potential, achieve personal fulfillment, and lead meaningful lives in an increasingly digital world. Join us as we explore the transformative potential of AI in personal development and self-improvement, shaping the future of human potential and well-being.

AI as a Tool for Personal Growth

Artificial Intelligence (AI) has emerged as a powerful tool for personal growth, offering innovative solutions to facilitate self-discovery, skill development, and holistic well-being. In this comprehensive exploration, we delve into the multifaceted ways in which AI is transforming personal growth and self-improvement, empowering individuals to unlock their full potential and lead fulfilling lives.

Personalized Learning and Skill Development

AI-driven platforms revolutionize the way individuals learn and develop new skills, tailoring educational content and experiences to their unique preferences and learning styles.

Adaptive Learning Systems: AI algorithms analyze individual learning behaviors and preferences to personalize educational content, pacing, and assessments, ensuring optimal engagement and retention of knowledge.

Skill Assessment and Recommendations: AI-powered platforms assess individuals' current skill levels and learning gaps, providing personalized recommendations for courses, tutorials, and learning resources to address their specific needs and goals.

Health and Wellness Management

AI technologies play a crucial role in promoting physical, mental, and emotional well-being, providing personalized insights and recommendations to support individuals' holistic health and self-care.

Health Monitoring and Analysis: AI-driven health and wellness apps track individuals' physical activity, sleep patterns, and physiological indicators, analyzing data to identify trends, patterns, and areas for improvement in their overall health and wellness.

Emotional Intelligence Development: AI applications facilitate the development of emotional intelligence through mindfulness exercises, mood tracking, and virtual coaching, helping individuals cultivate self-awareness, empathy, and resilience in their daily lives.

Productivity Enhancement and Time Management

AI tools assist individuals in optimizing their productivity and managing their time more effectively, enabling them to achieve their goals and fulfill their potential in both personal and professional domains.

Task Management and Automation: AI-powered task management tools prioritize tasks, schedule reminders, and automate routine activities, allowing individuals to focus their time and energy on high-value tasks and activities that align with their goals and priorities.

Intelligent Scheduling: AI algorithms analyze individuals' schedules, preferences, and priorities to suggest optimal times for meetings, appointments, and activities, minimizing conflicts and maximizing productivity throughout the day.

Goal Setting and Habit Formation

AI-driven platforms and apps support individuals in setting meaningful goals, tracking progress, and cultivating positive habits for personal and professional growth.

Goal Tracking and Progress Monitoring: AI-powered goal-setting platforms track individuals' progress towards their goals, providing real-time feedback and insights to keep them motivated and on track to achieve success.

Habit Tracking and Reinforcement: AI-driven habit-tracking apps monitor individuals' daily routines and behaviors, providing personalized feedback and incentives to reinforce positive habits and behaviors and overcome challenges or setbacks along the way.

Personalized Coaching and Mentorship

AI technologies offer virtual coaching and mentorship experiences tailored to individuals' unique needs, preferences, and aspirations, providing guidance, support, and accountability on their journey of personal growth and self-improvement.

Virtual Coaches and Mentors: AI-powered virtual coaching platforms leverage natural language processing and conversational interfaces to provide personalized guidance, advice, and encouragement to individuals seeking support in areas such as career development, leadership skills, and personal relationships.

Feedback and Reflection: AI-driven coaching and mentoring experiences facilitate self-reflection and self-awareness, encouraging individuals to assess their strengths, weaknesses, and areas for growth, and to develop actionable strategies for improvement.

Ethical and Social Considerations

While AI offers significant opportunities for personal growth and self-improvement, its integration into these domains also raises important ethical and social considerations that must be addressed to ensure responsible and equitable use of AI technologies.

Privacy and Data Security: AI technologies often rely on access to personal data, raising concerns about privacy, data security, and potential misuse or unauthorized access to sensitive information. Governments, organizations, and developers must establish robust data protection measures and safeguards to protect individuals' privacy rights and ensure the responsible use of personal data in AI-driven personal growth applications.

Algorithmic Bias and Fairness: AI algorithms may exhibit bias or discrimination against certain individuals or groups, leading to unfair or inequitable outcomes in personal growth and self-improvement processes. Addressing algorithmic bias requires transparency, accountability, and ongoing monitoring and evaluation of AI systems to ensure fairness and equity in their recommendations and decision-making processes.

Artificial Intelligence is transforming personal growth and self-improvement, offering innovative solutions to empower individuals to unlock their full potential and lead fulfilling lives. By leveraging AI technologies for personalized learning, health and wellness management, productivity enhancement, goal setting, personalized coaching, and mentorship, individuals can cultivate the skills, habits, and mindsets needed to thrive in an increasingly complex and fast-paced world. However, addressing ethical, privacy, and algorithmic bias considerations is essential to ensure responsible and equitable use of AI technologies in personal growth and self-improvement domains. As individuals embrace AI as a tool for personal growth, they must prioritize ethical and responsible AI governance to protect their privacy, autonomy, and well-being, and to promote inclusivity, fairness, and equity in their personal development journeys.g

The Future of Personalized Learning and Self-Optimization

Personalized learning and self-optimization are poised to undergo transformative advancements with the integration of Artificial Intelligence (AI) technologies. As we look ahead, the convergence of AI-driven platforms, data analytics, and cognitive science promises to revolutionize the way individuals learn, grow, and optimize their lives. In this in-depth exploration, we delve into the future of personalized learning and self-optimization, envisioning the possibilities and implications of AI-driven innovations in these domains.

Personalized Learning:

Personalized learning has already begun to reshape education, offering tailored experiences that cater to individual needs, preferences, and learning styles. Looking forward, AI will further refine and enhance personalized learning by:

Adaptive Curriculum: AI algorithms will dynamically adapt educational content and activities based on learners' progress, knowledge gaps, and learning preferences. This adaptive approach ensures that learners receive content at their optimal level of challenge, maximizing engagement and knowledge retention.

Intelligent Tutoring Systems: AI-powered tutoring systems will provide personalized support and guidance to learners, offering real-time feedback, explanations, and hints tailored to their individual learning needs. These intelligent tutors will adapt their teaching strategies based on learners' responses and performance, fostering deeper understanding and mastery of concepts.

Lifelong Learning Platforms: AI-driven lifelong learning platforms will offer personalized learning experiences beyond traditional educational settings, enabling individuals to pursue continuous skill development and personal growth throughout their lives. These platforms will curate diverse learning resources, recommend relevant courses and materials, and track learners' progress across various domains.

Self-Optimization:

Self-optimization involves leveraging data and insights to improve various aspects of one's life, including health, productivity, and well-being. With AI, self-optimization will evolve in the following ways:

Health and Wellness Monitoring: AI-powered health and wellness apps will provide individuals with personalized insights and recommendations to optimize their physical and mental well-being. These apps will analyze data from wearable devices, health trackers, and self-reported information to identify trends, patterns, and areas for improvement in individuals' lifestyles and habits.

Productivity and Time Management: AI tools will assist individuals in optimizing their productivity and managing their time more effectively. These tools will analyze users' schedules, priorities, and work habits to suggest strategies for better time allocation, task prioritization, and goal setting, enabling individuals to achieve greater efficiency and effectiveness in their daily activities.

Emotional Intelligence Development: AI-driven emotional intelligence (EI) platforms will offer personalized interventions and exercises to help individuals enhance their self-awareness, empathy, and resilience. These platforms will leverage AI algorithms to analyze users' emotional responses and provide targeted feedback and guidance for managing stress, improving communication, and building healthy relationships.

The Role of AI in Personal Growth:

AI will play a central role in facilitating personal growth and self-improvement by:

Tailored Interventions: AI algorithms will identify personalized interventions and strategies for individuals to overcome challenges, achieve goals, and realize their full potential. These interventions may include personalized learning plans, behavior change techniques, and wellness strategies tailored to individuals' unique needs and circumstances.

Continuous Feedback Loop: AI-driven feedback mechanisms will provide individuals with continuous feedback and insights on their progress, performance, and areas for improvement. This feedback loop will enable individuals to make informed decisions, adjust their strategies, and track their growth journey over time.

Predictive Analytics: AI-powered predictive analytics will forecast future trends, opportunities, and challenges in individuals' lives, enabling proactive decision-making and planning. By analyzing historical data and patterns, AI algorithms will anticipate potential obstacles and recommend preventive measures to help individuals navigate life's uncertainties more effectively.

Ethical and Social Implications:

As AI becomes more integrated into personalized learning and self-optimization processes, several ethical and social considerations must be addressed:

Privacy and Data Security: AI-driven platforms must prioritize user privacy and data security, ensuring that individuals have control over their personal information and how it is used. Transparent data practices, informed consent mechanisms, and robust security measures are essential to safeguarding users' privacy rights.

Algorithmic Bias and Fairness: AI algorithms must be developed and trained to mitigate biases and ensure fairness in personalized recommendations and interventions. Ethical AI design principles, diversity in training data, and regular audits are critical to minimizing algorithmic bias and promoting equitable outcomes for all users.

Digital Divide: Access to AI-driven personalized learning and self-optimization tools must be equitable and inclusive, addressing disparities in digital literacy, access to technology, and socio-economic status. Efforts to bridge the digital divide and promote digital inclusion are essential to ensuring that everyone can benefit from AI-driven innovations in personal growth and well-being.

The future of personalized learning and self-optimization holds tremendous promise, fueled by advancements in AI technologies and data-driven insights. By leveraging AI to tailor educational experiences, enhance well-being, and support personal growth, individuals can unlock their full potential and lead more fulfilling lives. However, realizing this vision requires a thoughtful approach to addressing ethical, privacy, and equity considerations, ensuring that AI-driven innovations in personal development are responsible, inclusive, and empowering for all. As we embrace the transformative potential of AI in personalized learning and self-optimization, we must strive to create a future where technology serves as a catalyst for human flourishing and well-being.

AI in Fitness and Wellness: Revolutionizing Health and Well-Being

In recent years, Artificial Intelligence (AI) has emerged as a game-changer in the field of fitness and wellness. From personalized workout plans to advanced health monitoring systems, AI technologies are transforming how individuals approach their health and well-being. In this comprehensive exploration, we delve into the multifaceted ways in which AI is revolutionizing fitness and wellness.

Personalized Fitness Programs

AI-driven platforms are reshaping personalized fitness programs by leveraging data analytics and machine learning algorithms to tailor workout routines and nutrition plans to individuals' unique needs, preferences, and goals.

Data-driven Insights: AI algorithms analyze data from wearable fitness trackers, smart devices, and user feedback to assess individuals' fitness levels, activity patterns, and dietary habits. This data is then used to generate personalized recommendations for exercise routines, dietary guidelines, and lifestyle modifications.

Adaptive Workouts: AI-powered fitness apps adapt workout routines in real-time based on users' performance, feedback, and progress. By adjusting intensity, duration, and exercises according to users' abilities and goals, these apps maximize effectiveness and minimize the risk of injury.

Virtual Coaching and Training

AI technologies offer virtual coaching and training experiences that provide personalized guidance, motivation, and support to individuals on their fitness journey.

Virtual Personal Trainers: AI-powered virtual personal trainers deliver customized workout sessions, exercise demonstrations, and real-time feedback through interactive platforms. These virtual trainers adapt their coaching style and intensity based on users' preferences, fitness levels, and performance metrics.

Nutritional Coaching: AI-driven nutrition apps provide personalized meal plans, recipe suggestions, and dietary recommendations tailored to users' nutritional needs, dietary preferences, and fitness goals. These apps track users' food intake, analyze nutritional content, and offer insights to help individuals make healthier choices and achieve their dietary objectives.

Health Monitoring and Management

AI technologies facilitate proactive health monitoring and management, empowering individuals to track, analyze, and optimize their health metrics in real-time.

Biometric Tracking: Wearable fitness devices equipped with AI algorithms monitor users' biometric data, including heart rate, sleep patterns, and stress levels. By analyzing this data, these devices provide insights into users' overall health and well-being, alerting them to potential health risks and prompting them to take preventive action.

Health Predictions: AI-powered health monitoring systems use predictive analytics to forecast individuals' health trajectories and identify potential health issues before they arise. By analyzing historical data, lifestyle factors, and genetic predispositions, these systems offer personalized recommendations for preventive care, early intervention, and disease management.

Enhanced User Engagement and Motivation

AI-driven fitness and wellness apps enhance user engagement and motivation, fostering adherence to healthy habits and behaviors over the long term.

Gamification: AI-powered fitness apps incorporate gamification elements, such as challenges, rewards, and social interactions, to make exercise more enjoyable and engaging. By turning fitness into a game, these apps motivate users to stay active, set new goals, and track their progress in a fun and interactive way.

Behavioral Insights: AI algorithms analyze users' behavior patterns, motivational triggers, and psychological factors to identify strategies for enhancing engagement and adherence to fitness goals. By understanding users' motivations and barriers to exercise, AI-driven apps offer personalized interventions and incentives to keep users motivated and on track.

Ethical and Privacy Considerations

As AI technologies become increasingly integrated into fitness and wellness applications, it is essential to address ethical and privacy considerations to ensure responsible and equitable use of these technologies.

Data Privacy: AI-powered fitness apps must prioritize user privacy and data security, ensuring that individuals have control over their personal information and how it is used. Transparent data practices, informed consent mechanisms, and robust security measures are essential to safeguarding users' privacy rights.

Algorithmic Bias: AI algorithms used in fitness and wellness applications must be trained on diverse and representative datasets to minimize bias and ensure fairness in personalized recommendations and interventions. Ethical AI design principles, diversity in training data, and regular audits are critical to mitigating algorithmic bias and promoting equitable outcomes for all users.

Artificial Intelligence is reshaping the fitness and wellness industry, offering innovative solutions to help individuals achieve their health and fitness goals, optimize their well-being, and lead healthier lifestyles. By leveraging AI for personalized fitness programs, virtual coaching and training, health monitoring and management, enhanced user engagement, and motivation, individuals can take control of their health and well-being like never before. However, addressing ethical, privacy, and algorithmic bias considerations is essential to ensure that AI-driven innovations in fitness and wellness promote responsible, inclusive, and empowering experiences for all users. As we embrace the transformative potential of AI in fitness and wellness, we must prioritize ethical and responsible AI governance to protect users' privacy, autonomy, and well-being and to promote equitable access to health and fitness resources for everyone.

AI in Fitness and Wellness: Enhancing Health and Well-being

In recent years, Artificial Intelligence (AI) has emerged as a game-changer in the field of fitness and wellness, offering innovative solutions to help individuals lead healthier and more active lifestyles. By leveraging AI technologies, fitness enthusiasts and health-conscious individuals can access personalized workout plans, receive real-time feedback on their progress, and make more informed decisions about their overall well-being. In this detailed exploration, we will delve into the multifaceted ways in which AI is revolutionizing fitness and wellness.

Personalized Fitness Plans

One of the most significant impacts of AI in fitness and wellness is the ability to create personalized workout plans tailored to individual needs and preferences. AI algorithms analyze data from wearable fitness trackers, user input, and medical records to develop customized exercise routines that take into account factors such as fitness level, goals, and any existing health conditions. These personalized plans not only maximize the effectiveness of workouts but also minimize the risk of injury by adapting to the user's abilities in real-time.

Intelligent Coaching and Feedback

AI-powered coaching platforms provide users with intelligent feedback and guidance to optimize their workouts and achieve their fitness goals. These platforms use machine learning algorithms to analyze performance data, identify areas for improvement, and offer personalized recommendations for training intensity, exercise selection, and recovery strategies. Additionally, virtual coaches can provide real-time feedback during workouts, correcting form errors and motivating users to push themselves further.

Health Monitoring and Analysis

AI plays a crucial role in health monitoring and analysis, enabling users to track key health metrics and identify trends over time. Wearable fitness devices equipped with AI algorithms can monitor factors such as heart rate variability, sleep quality, and stress levels, providing users with insights into their overall well-being. By analyzing this data, users can gain a better understanding of their health status and make informed decisions about their lifestyle habits and behaviors.

Nutrition Guidance and Meal Planning

In addition to fitness, AI technologies are also being used to improve nutrition guidance and meal planning. AI-powered apps can analyze dietary preferences, nutritional requirements, and food preferences to generate personalized meal plans that align with the user's health and fitness goals. These apps can also provide real-time feedback on meal choices, helping users make healthier decisions and maintain a balanced diet.

Predictive Analytics and Preventive Health

AI-driven predictive analytics enable users to anticipate and prevent health issues before they arise. By analyzing historical health data and lifestyle factors, AI algorithms can identify patterns and risk factors associated with certain health conditions, allowing users to take proactive measures to mitigate their risk. For example, AI-powered apps can alert users to potential health concerns based on changes in their activity levels, sleep patterns, or vital signs, prompting them to seek medical attention or adjust their behavior accordingly.

Ethical Considerations and Privacy

While AI offers tremendous potential to improve fitness and wellness, it also raises important ethical considerations, particularly concerning data privacy and algorithmic bias. Users must trust that their personal data will be handled responsibly and securely, and that AI algorithms will provide unbiased and accurate recommendations. Additionally, there is a need for greater transparency and accountability in the development and deployment of AI-powered fitness and wellness solutions to ensure that they are accessible and inclusive for all users.

In conclusion, AI is revolutionizing the way we approach fitness and wellness by providing personalized guidance, intelligent coaching, and predictive analytics to help individuals achieve their health and fitness goals. By harnessing the power of AI, we can empower individuals to lead healthier, more active lifestyles and improve their overall well-being. However, it is essential to address ethical considerations and privacy concerns to ensure that AI technologies are used responsibly and ethically in the pursuit of better health for all.

AI and the Quest for Life Balance: Leveraging Technology for Well-being

In an era marked by rapid technological advancements and increasing demands on our time and attention, the quest for life balance has become more elusive than ever. As we navigate the complexities of modern life, Artificial Intelligence (AI) is emerging as a powerful ally in our pursuit of well-being, offering innovative solutions to help us manage our time, reduce stress, and foster greater harmony in our lives. In this in-depth exploration, we will delve into the multifaceted ways in which AI is reshaping our approach to life balance and enhancing our overall quality of life.

Understanding Life Balance

Before we delve into the role of AI in fostering life balance, it's essential to define what we mean by this term. Life balance refers to the equilibrium we strive to achieve between various aspects of our lives, including work, family, health, relationships, and personal interests. Achieving life balance involves managing competing priorities, setting boundaries, and allocating time and energy in a way that aligns with our values and goals.

AI-Powered Time Management

One of the most significant challenges in maintaining life balance is effectively managing our time. AI-powered time management tools offer valuable assistance in this regard, helping us prioritize tasks, optimize our schedules, and make the most of our limited time.

Smart Scheduling: AI algorithms analyze our calendars, commitments, and preferences to suggest optimal times for meetings, appointments, and tasks. By automating the scheduling process, these tools help us avoid double bookings, minimize downtime, and ensure that our time is allocated efficiently.

Task Prioritization: AI-powered task management apps use machine learning algorithms to prioritize our to-do lists based on factors such as deadlines, importance, and estimated completion times. By focusing on high-priority tasks and delegating or deferring less critical ones, we can make better use of our time and reduce feelings of overwhelm.

Stress Reduction and Mental Health Support

In our fast-paced world, stress and mental health issues are significant barriers to achieving life balance. AI-driven mental health apps and chatbots provide accessible and personalized support to help us manage stress, anxiety, and other mental health challenges.

Emotional Intelligence: AI algorithms analyze our communication patterns, tone of voice, and facial expressions to assess our emotional state and provide personalized recommendations for stress management and self-care. These tools offer coping strategies, relaxation techniques, and mindfulness exercises tailored to our individual needs.

24/7 Support: AI-powered chatbots and virtual assistants offer round-the-clock support for individuals experiencing stress or mental health concerns. By providing empathetic listening, supportive responses, and evidence-based interventions, these bots offer a valuable lifeline for those in need of immediate assistance.

Enhancing Work-Life Integration

Achieving a healthy balance between work and personal life is essential for overall well-being. AI technologies facilitate work-life integration by providing flexible work arrangements, remote collaboration tools, and productivity-enhancing solutions.

Remote Work Solutions: AI-powered collaboration platforms enable remote teams to work efficiently and effectively from anywhere in the world. These platforms offer features such as video conferencing, document sharing, and project management tools to facilitate seamless communication and collaboration.

Workflow Automation: AI algorithms automate repetitive tasks, streamline workflows, and reduce administrative overhead, allowing us to focus on more meaningful and fulfilling aspects of our work and personal lives. By delegating routine tasks to AI, we can reclaim valuable time and energy for activities that matter most to us.

Personalized Wellness and Self-Care

Maintaining physical health and well-being is an essential component of life balance. AI-driven wellness apps and devices offer personalized recommendations, insights, and support to help us prioritize self-care and make healthier lifestyle choices.

Health Tracking: Wearable fitness trackers equipped with AI algorithms monitor our activity levels, sleep patterns, and vital signs, providing valuable insights into our overall health and well-being. These devices offer personalized recommendations for exercise, nutrition, and sleep hygiene to help us maintain optimal health.

Nutrition Guidance: AI-powered nutrition apps analyze our dietary habits, preferences, and goals to generate personalized meal plans, recipe suggestions, and nutritional recommendations. By tracking our food intake and providing real-time feedback, these apps help us make healthier choices and maintain a balanced diet.

Ethical Considerations and Privacy

As we embrace AI technologies to enhance our well-being and achieve life balance, it's essential to consider the ethical implications and privacy concerns associated with these tools.

Data Privacy: AI-powered wellness apps and devices collect sensitive personal data, including health information and biometric measurements. It's crucial to ensure that this data is handled responsibly, securely, and in accordance with relevant privacy regulations to protect users' confidentiality and autonomy.

Algorithmic Bias: AI algorithms used in wellness applications must be trained on diverse and representative datasets to avoid perpetuating biases and disparities in health outcomes. It's essential to conduct regular audits, monitor for bias, and implement corrective measures to ensure that AI-driven wellness solutions are fair, equitable, and inclusive for all users.

In conclusion, AI has the potential to play a transformative role in our quest for life balance by providing personalized support, optimizing our time, and fostering greater well-being. By leveraging AI technologies responsibly and ethically, we can harness the power of technology to enhance our quality of life, reduce stress, and cultivate greater harmony and fulfillment in all aspects of our lives. As we navigate the complexities of modern life, AI serves as a valuable ally in our ongoing pursuit of well-being and life balance.

www.ingramcontent.com/pod-product-compliance
Lightning Source LLC
LaVergne TN
LVHW061552070526
838199LV00077B/7018